HELP YO
WITH TH
NEW MAT

In the same series

555 Ways to Amuse a Child
Children's Party and Games Book

Uniform with this book

HELP YOUR CHILD WITH THE NEW MATHS

by

CLAUDE BIRTWISTLE

(Former Senior Mathematics Adviser to Lancashire County Council)

PAPERFRONTS

ELLIOT RIGHT WAY BOOKS

KINGSWOOD SURREY UK

Made and printed in Great Britain by
Love and Malcomson, Redhill, Surrey.

CONTENTS

1
INTRODUCTION

It is the purpose of this book to explain to parents the mathematics which is taught in primary schools today. Over the past two or three decades there have been many changes in the subjects taught in our schools and in the ways of teaching. These changes arose partly to meet the demands of a new technological society and partly as a result of changing ideas about how children learn. Nowhere have they been more marked than in the teaching of mathematics.

Parents may find difficulty in understanding the changes and in appreciating what is taking place. Most parents are anxious to help their children to make progress in their school work and to assist with difficulties. But this is not always easy! The parent finds the new work strange and the child, anxious for help, often finds the parent's explanation different from what has been taught in school and, possibly, even creating more difficulties of understanding.

At the outset it is necessary to reassure the parent. 'New' or 'modern' mathematics has made its appearance and is taught in many schools. Some schools use published textbooks, so we even hear of things like 'Fletcher Maths', 'Nuffield Maths' and 'S.M.P. Maths'. Other schools will say that they are not doing a 'modern mathematics' course, but are following a 'traditional' course.

It would be difficult to say briefly what the 'new' courses have in common. They probably incorporate a different approach from that of the past, with more emphasis on handling materials and performing tasks which lead to the build-up of mathematical ideas, and the work covers shape, graphs and easy statistics, integrated with the more usual topics of arithmetic.

But it is no easier to say what is meant by 'traditional' courses of mathematics. Those who claim to be teaching such a course would say that they put particular emphasis on calculation practice, perhaps, but even here what is taught differs from what was taught in mathematics lessons of twenty-five or more years ago.

The truth is that there is only one mathematics, but it is a vast subject and schools may choose to teach and emphasize different aspects, although all will cover certain basic work. A school which only taught arithmetic skills would be neglecting the important geometrical, graphical and statistical ideas which children up to the age of twelve should meet. On the other hand, if a school taught 'new' topics without taking care to develop number skills and systematic thought in its pupils, it would be equally guilty of giving them an inadequate mathematical education.

Schools, therefore, provide the type of mathematical course which they feel is suited best to their own circumstances. Many factors are taken into consideration. For example, the topics which appeal to the interests and abilities of these particular children, and the type of mathematics which is taught in the secondary school to which the children are going.

One result of this freedom of choice is that there is no common course taught by all schools. Of late there have been moves to try to bring about some degree of standardisation within particular areas, but not in the country as a whole. Such freedom has both advantages and disadvantages. One obvious benefit is that schools are able to suit their work to their assessment of the child's needs. On the other hand, a child changing schools as the parents move to a job in a new area, can have difficulty in understanding the work in the new school. This can be particularly so in mathematics, where new work is often built on earlier work, which the child may not have done in his previous school because of the difference in the courses.

In such circumstances, the parent may wish to help his child with mathematics, but of course many other parents are equally keen to give their children assistance under more normal circumstances. It is the aim of this book to assist parents to understand the mathematics being taught to their children, whether they are covering a 'modern' or a 'traditional' syllabus. The newer topics are covered and so are the well-established ones, although parents may find that the treatment of the latter differs from that employed when they were at school. So the 'new maths' of our title means the mathematics being taught in the schools today.

The ways in which the subject is taught are outlined so that parents may understand the different approaches used in schools. When helping a child it is important to use the methods he has been taught at school. This point will be stressed later. In the book, alternative methods are sometimes given and the parent should choose those with which the child is familiar. There are suggestions on how to overcome particular difficulties, but parents may be able to devise other means depending on the needs of the individual child. In particular, Chapter 3 sets out the general principles for helping a child with mathematics.

HOW TO USE THE BOOK

It is suggested that the best method to use the book is:

1. You, the parent, should read the book carefully, to get an overall understanding of the work and how it is taught. As far as possible, try to relate it to what, and how, you were taught, so that you may have a better understanding.

2. Subsequently use the index of the book to find individual topics on which you wish to help your child. The index also includes different terms used in mathematics and states where those are explained in the text. Certain topics are explained in more detail in Chapter 11.

3. If possible, look at the books or work-cards which your child is using at school, try to identify the methods being used there and relate them to the relevant sections of the book.

SPECIAL NOTE

To save repetition, the word 'his' will be used when referring to a pupil in the general sense and should be taken to mean 'his or her'. Under no circumstances must this be interpreted as subscribing to the myth that mathematics is not a girl's subject!

2

CHANGING IDEAS ON MATHEMATICAL EDUCATION

The system of universal elementary education that originated in the nineteenth century had arithemetic as one of the 3 R's which, along with religious education, made up the curriculum. Since that time, whatever changes have taken place in our schools, the study of language and the study of arithmetic (or mathematics) have – quite rightly – remained as the basic subjects. In the early days the arithmetic that was taught was simple basic calculation whose purpose was to provide a grounding in the four rules: addition, subtraction, multiplication and division. The aim was to provide people with a working knowledge of simple money, and other, calculations which they would meet in their everyday life.

Gradually this basic education in arithmetic was extended. Changes in society brought about by increased industrial and commercial activity involved people in more complex mathematical calculations. Nevertheless, the method of teaching mathematics remained very much one of teaching particular techniques. We were shown how to do a problem, e.g. one tap fills a bath in 5 minutes and the other tap fills it in 4 minutes; if both taps were turned on, how long to fill the bath? Then we were asked to do a similar problem, possibly where one tap took 6 minutes and the other 8 minutes. There are textbooks full of examples for use in this type of teaching technique.

In the 1950's many industrialists began to express concern about the mathematical abilities of young people who came to them from schools and colleges. Their main complaint was that, whereas many of these young people were able to perform calculations on textbook problems, they were incapable of using their mathematics in real life situations. In other words, although they may have been able to do certain calculations provided they knew which calculation was required, they were unable to take an everyday problem, analyse it in terms of mathematics and thereby find a solution.

It was as a result of such criticism and general concern about mathematical standards in an increasingly technological society that changes took place, and are still taking place, in what mathematics is taught in our schools. The move has been from arithmetic which was concerned mainly with calculation, to mathematics which studies relationships and calculations arising from quantity, shape, statistical information and other sources. The emphasis, too, has changed from learning how to do particular types of examples, to knowing how to seek one's own solution to real problems. The change has been twofold: a change in *what* is taught and a change in *how* it is taught.

WHY DO WE NEED TO STUDY MATHEMATICS?

In answering this question, three possible levels of requirement may be identified:

(a) we need it for everyday use;

(b) we need it for our job;

(c) we need it for a study of mathematics as a discipline.

Clearly, not everyone needs to study for each of these categories; taking (b), for example, some jobs require a wide knowledge of the subject, whereas others may require very little. Everyday use, of course, is something which concerns everyone and life today calls for more mathematical background than it did in the past. Wages, mortgages, H.P., taxes and similar everyday topics require some mathematical understanding. The increasing use of computers which present results in mathematical form, and large amounts of other information which has a mathematical basis, call for a background in the subject if the individual is to be able to deal intelligently and responsibly with the facts of present-day life.

The third category, the study of mathematics as a discipline, is one which concerns the specialist particularly, i.e. those who are to make a career out of mathematics or its allied subjects. It is worth noting, however, that the demand for such people is increasing and many more will be undertaking such studies in the future. Also, even at lower levels, there are advantages to be gained from a study of the subject for the training it gives in the areas of logical reasoning and understanding.

NEW SCHEMES OF WORK

Broadening the mathematical curriculum meant the introduction of new topics. In the main this was done for two reasons. The first was to create interest in the subject. New topics could stimulate thought, could show mathematics in real situations and could encourage better understanding of basic techniques. Secondly, the introduction of new work and different language in the subject could produce more precision so that ideas became clearer, and also lead to better understanding.

As was pointed out in the Introduction, there is a wide variation between schools as to how far they have gone with the introduction of such new topics. Most schools have a scheme of work which lays down what should be taught in the school. Often these schemes are made up by the staff based on those topics which they feel are best suited to their circumstances and the needs of their pupils, and considerable thought and time has to be devoted to drawing up such a scheme. Other schools feel that their needs are best met by some published scheme which they have decided on after careful comparisons of many such schemes available.

Some of the published schemes are based on pupil books which incorporate ideas for practical work as well as the more usual practice examples. Other schemes consist of individual work cards, again containing both practical work and practice problems. Some schools write and duplicate their own worksheets. Whichever method is used, however, pupils in most schools are now involved in some practical work in the mathematics lesson. This leads to a consideration of newer ways of teaching the subject.

NEW METHODS OF TEACHING

One of the misconceptions that people have about the new mathematics is that calculation techniques are either no longer taught or are inadequately taught. It should be stressed at once that one cannot have mathematics without calculation and so these techniques are just as important as they have always been. However, there are two important points. Children should understand the calculation processes they use and calculation should relate to real life and not be 'calculation for calculation's sake'.

There seems little purpose in knowing calculation techniques if one does not know which technique to use in any particular circumstance. A simple and true instance will illustrate. A boy was required to estimate the length in feet of the classroom without using a ruler. How could he do it? he was asked. He said he could pace it out. How long was his pace? About a yard, he replied. He performed the task and said it was 12 yards long. But the answer is required in feet; how many feet are there in a yard? Three, he replied. Very good, then what is the length of the room in feet? A few moments thought and then he replied, 15 feet. Now the working was correct, since $12 + 3 = 15$; unfortunately he had used the wrong technique, adding instead of multiplying.

This difficulty of knowing techniques but not how to use them, has led to changes in the way the subject is taught, with an increased emphasis on practical approaches. It is important for the child to see how mathematical problems arise. 'Add three and two and the answer is five' is a mathematical fact, but the child needs to see this fact with three pencils and two pencils, three pennies and two pennies and so on, so that some meaning is attached to the abstract fact, $3+2=5$.

The ability to use mathematics is equally important. By this is meant not just the ability to perform a calculation identical to one that has just been done, but to meet a new problem and find an appropriate method of getting an answer. To take a simple example, suppose we have four rows of cabbages with eight in a row, how do we find the total number of cabbages? Are they counted: 1, 2, 3, 4, . . ., 31, 32 or do we notice the arrangement and mulitiply 4 by 8?

Whereas in the past, a problem in mathematics was worked through on the blackboard and the children then did similar problems, nowadays there is often a great deal of activity and discussion before doing practice examples from a book or work card. Some of these examples may be designed to make the pupil seek his own method of solution. Sometimes there may be no single answer to an example, but it is left to the pupil to give his own individual answer. The emphasis is on children learning and using mathematics. Although this leads to better understanding, it often means that more time is taken at initial stages of the work and there is less to show in actual written work in an exercise book than there was under the old 'teach a technique' system. Sometimes this causes concern to parents who feel that John or Mary is not doing as much work as he or she should be! The real test of whether this is, or is not so, lies not in the number of worked examples, but in the depth of understanding of the individual child.

HOW UNDERSTANDING IS BUILT UP

Suppose you wished to teach a child what is meant by 'red'. You would show him a succession of objects which were red – a book, a dress, a shoe and so on. Gradually he would be able to extract the common property of 'red' from these different objects. You would then get him to apply his knowledge by showing you other objects which were red and also objects which were not red. The idea of 'redness' which the child now develops is called a *concept*. Such basic ideas cannot be taught; they can only come through experience. How could you teach what is meant by 'red' without showing objects which are red? A blind person cannot know what red means.

In mathematics, the numbers are basic concepts. Just as the child needs experience to know what is meant by 'red', so he needs experience to know what is meant by 'two'. Many a proud mother brings her child to the infant school as a new entrant and tells the teacher 'he can count up to 20' and then makes him recite the numbers in order. Unfortunately when you ask him to bring five pencils from the table he cannot perform the task. He has been taught some words but he does not know what they mean.

Returning to the example of the concept of red, suppose you now wish to teach a child what is meant by 'colour'. As before, where the idea of redness was abstracted from many different situations, so the idea of colour has to come from a variety of experiences. Before 'colour' is understood, the child has to understand 'red', 'yellow', 'blue', 'green' and so on. In other words the concept of colour is built on these earlier concepts. If 'red', 'yellow' and so on are said to be concepts of the first order, then colour is a second order concept.

The same applies in mathematics. Numbers such as 'two' and 'three' are first order concepts, but when we 'add' them we are introducing a second order concept, since the idea of adding is built on the earlier concept of number. Third, fourth and even higher orders of concepts are involved in mathematical work as more complex calculations are built on earlier ones. It should now be apparent that if a child fails to obtain a thorough understanding of earlier concepts, he will be unable to build later concepts on that understanding and is likely to have difficulty with his work in mathematics.

Many of these later ideas which are acquired are developed into *techniques* and very frequently we use such techniques without really thinking about the underlying reasons for them. A simple example is with multiplication tables. For instance, we learn that three fours are twelve and use this fact repeatedly without thinking that what we are really doing is using a quick way to add three fours. The use of such techniques is quite in order; why then do we need to worry about understanding the way in which we have obtained them? The answer lies in the correct application of the techniques. If we do not understand what they really imply, then we either fail to recognize that we can solve a problem by using a particular technique or we employ the wrong technique and obtain a wrong solution. The case of the boy mentioned earlier who was finding the length of a room, is an example of the latter. He probably knew the multiplication tables, but failed to see that the particular problem called for their use.

Once a technique has been developed, it is important that practice is given in the use of that technique in a wide variety of situations. Still using the example of multiplication tables, the practice would include the application of multiplication in a wide variety of problems of different types. A simple illustration is: How many cabbages in 4 rows with 8 in a row? What is the cost of 4 oranges at 8 pence each? How long is a piece of string which can be cut exactly into 4 lengths, each 8 cm long? These examples all depend on multiplying 4 by 8, but use it in different circumstances.

The importance of the work on *application* of techniques is that it brings a broader understanding of the principles involved and encourages analysis of problems to try to find ways of solving them. This habit of thought is one which should be encouraged, even with young children. Instead of a child being told how to solve a problem, he should be helped to seek his own way to a solution.

We shall return to these points when we consider, in the next chapter, ways in which parents can help their children. It may be useful at this point to summarize these ideas applied to the learning of mathematics.

The work should start with *activity* based on *real material.* This could be measuring things, using counting apparatus, drawing, handling shapes, etc. This should lead to *discussion*, where the child is encouraged to think about certain aspects of what he is doing and also encouraged to put his thoughts into words. This can lead to further activity ('what would happen if . . . ?) and more discussion ('why do you think that is so?). The next step is the *consolidation* of the ideas that have been developed. This is the point where the techniques are practised and the work is set down in writing (e.g. addition sums, multiplications). Finally comes the *application* of these techniques to new situations so that the correct use is understood.

Two points in the last paragraph need amplification: discussion and setting down of work. Mathematics is a language; it is a specialised form of English. Symbols are used as shorthand, but they do represent words, and mathematical sentences are (or should be) just as grammatical as sentences in ordinary English. $3+4=7$ can be read as a correct English sentence: 'Three added to four is equal to seven'. It is important, therefore, that children be encouraged to express themselves clearly in mathematics. The first stage of this process is through discussion. Next, when written work is being done, this needs to be set down in an orderly and 'grammatical' fashion.

To end this chapter, it may be useful to the parent to indicate some of the ways in which work is organized in schools. These are general methods and do not apply solely to the teaching of mathematics. The changed classroom approach is perhaps best summed up by the term '*child centred*' applied to the choice of curriculum and methods of learning. Such education puts the emphasis on individual development of each child and, by assessing each child's needs, determines the work that he or she does, how it is done and the rate of working. In some schools this leads to an *integrated day* or an *integrated curriculum*. With the former there is no fixed timetable of periods of the day devoted to certain subjects, but a flexible arrangement allows particular tasks or items of work to be completed before moving onto other work. In the case of an integrated curriculum, groups of subjects are taken together without any particular boundaries between them and such work can very often be *topic work* where a broad topic (e.g. transport) is used to provide a source of work in English, mathematics, history, geography, etc. *Discovery methods*, as the name implies, are where children are encouraged to investigate and find out for themselves. This does not mean that children are left to their own devices, for such work is carefully arranged and structured by the teacher to lead the child along certain lines of investigation, after which the teacher draws the work together into a formal conclusion.

Within a classroom, children may be working individually, in groups or as a whole class. With *individual working* every child is engaged on their own particular task; the other extreme is the *formal class lesson*, where all the children are gathered together before the teacher, doing the same work and frequently being taught from the blackboard. Another type of classroom organization is *group work*, where the class is split up into small groups of pupils. The groups may be arranged according to ability with the pupils in each group doing roughly the same work. At other times children in a group may be working together as a team on some large project. It does not follow that one of these different types of class organization – individual, group, or class teaching – is always employed all the time by a particular teacher. Some teachers favour one method rather than another, but usually a teacher will vary the methods according to circumstances, so that all three methods are used at different times.

In all matters of organization and methods of teaching it is usually fair to say that the teacher uses those best suited to individual circumstances, so that each child has the opportunity to develop his or her abilities to the fullest extent.

3
HELPING YOUR CHILD

The desire to help your child with his or her mathematics may arise in various ways, ranging from a general (and commendable!) interest to know what your child is doing, through a need to respond to a call for help with a particular problem or 'sum', to being faced with the situation of a child having grave difficulties with the subject as a whole. It is possible to give help to children in all such circumstances, but at the outset, the importance of co-operation with the school must be stressed.

In the last chapter, a brief summary was given of the many ways in which mathematics is taught in schools. Generally speaking, what is taught and how it is taught is the decision of that teacher for those particular children in the circumstances. As every parent will recognize, the help that is given has to fit in with the work of the school. The first step, then, is to be fully aware of what is being done at school. Go to the school, talk to the teachers, ask to see work that is being done. There are opportunities at parents' evenings, but, in most schools, parents are welcome to call at other times to discuss children's work. Try to understand what is being done at the school, although some of the work may seem strange to you – at times it might even seem pointless!

A prime essential is a child's attitude to the subject and it is here that a parent can have considerable influence. Words carelessly thrown out can have an adverse effect on a child. Often one hears adults say things like 'I could never do mathematics when I was at school!' in a tone of voice which implies that in any case it doesn't really matter. Unfortunately it *does* matter, particularly in present-day society. But if a parent says this to a child, one can imagine the child's response. It is important to encourage the child in his or her work. If one admits one's own failure with the subject, it should be with regret and the hope that the youngster will do better than oneself. The importance and value of mathematics in life should be pointed out; this was set out in the previous chapter. But there are lighter and enjoyable sides to the subject which can stimulate an interest and develop desirable attitudes. Mathematical puzzles and mathematical games are valuable in this respect; suggestions will be given later. Give every encouragement to the child; if he is doing something at school which you do not know or you have forgotten, have him explain it to you. This can give a sense of achievement, inspire self-confidence and help to clarify the child's own thinking.

OCCASIONAL HELP

Under this heading is the call for assistance when a child is stuck with a particular problem. This can happen because of a number of factors:

(a) Language. The child does not comprehend the problem. Mathematical problems are often stated in words and, although children can read the words, they may have difficulty in understanding what is being asked. Assistance in such cases consists of helping the child with the language; it is better if you can help him to understand what is written than simply re-stating the problem in different words. By so doing, you are helping in his understanding of English.

(b) Inability to relate to known methods. This usually occurs when techniques are being practised. The problem usually differs in some way from what has been done before and the application of the technique is not seen. In this case, go back to earlier examples and ask the child to explain what he has been doing and why. Then start to analyse the existing problem with him, helping him to break it down into parts until he sees some similarity with what has gone before, or sees a way in which he can tackle the problem.

(c) Failure to understand new work. The child has been introduced to some new topic and has failed completely to understand it. Remembering the principles outlined in the previous chapter, if possible go back to some practical situation which the child can see and handle (suggestions are made at appropriate sections in later chapters). Discuss the material with the child as he handles it; ask questions which will lead him to think about what he is doing. It is in these cases where the value of co-operation with the school becomes apparent, since you will have some idea of the way in which the school would approach the problem. Ask the child what he did in his lesson; try to envisage what was the purpose of the work. Either try to reconstruct the work or discuss what took place in class and help the child to extract the important parts. Follow this with other practical applications of the same principles, if you can think of some. For example, if number apparatus has been used at school, go over the work using coins or match-sticks as counters.

(d) Mistakes in techniques. These are dealt with in more detail in later chapters under appropriate headings. Causes range from simple carelessness to lack of understanding of basic principles. As an example, subtraction is a common source of difficulty. Difficulties arise from lack of understanding of place value (place value is explained in Chapter 5, page 48) and lead to figures being put in wrong columns, e.g. 6 + 15 is written

$$\begin{array}{r} 6 \\ +\ \underline{15} \\ 75 \end{array}$$

Common errors in subtraction include the case where the child always takes the smaller digit from the larger, as for example:

$$\begin{array}{r} 56 \\ -\ \underline{38} \\ 22 \end{array}$$

In such cases the child's thought should be directed to the basic principles, possibly with the use of some type of apparatus or physical representation of the problem.

CONTINUOUS DIFFICULTY WITH THE SUBJECT

There are children who have repeated difficulties with mathematics, there is a general failure to grasp principles, techniques are soon forgotten, new work presents further problems and, in general, the child develops a feeling of hopelessness in the subject. Such children are frequently put into remedial groups at school where the work is arranged on a special basis. Unfortunately not all such groups are a success; too frequently the work given is repeated exercises aimed at practising techniques, particularly the four rules of addition, subtraction, multiplication and division. What is really lacking, of course, is the basic understanding of concepts which underlie these techniques. This may have come about through absence from school at vital points in the teaching of the class, or through change of school, or through inattention at an appropriate point or the failure of the teacher to recognize that this particular child has not really understood.

Giving help to a child in these circumstances inevitably means a return to earlier work, including appropriate concrete experiences, e.g. handling things, counting things, adding them together and so on. In one way the parent is perhaps even better fitted to the task than the teacher, since it is possible to give the child this experience in his everyday world as he goes around the house, the garden or even travels around outside. The importance of language in mathematics has already been raised and the more mathematics can be brought into everyday activity, the better the understanding. Money, including shopping, is a typical example, but things like laying the table with cutlery, helping with weighing out ingredients for cooking, and telling the time, are valuable as sources of practical mathematics.

At the same time, do not forget games with a mathematical basis, e.g. Ludo, Snakes and Ladders, Dominoes,

Monopoly, and these do not have to be commercially produced games. For example, 'Odd or Even' is a game played with buttons or similar material. Each player starts with about 10 or 12 buttons. One player takes a number of his buttons in his closed hand and the other player has to guess whether there is an odd or even number in the hand. If he guesses correctly, he receives a button; if wrongly, he gives his opponent a button. The second player now takes a number of his buttons in his closed hand and the game proceeds in the same manner. The person to end up with all the buttons is the winner.

As the child develops confidence in dealing with numbers in real material, he should be encouraged to write down the working. It will be explained later how this work of *recording* should follow closely the steps in the working with the material. When dealing with a child having difficulty with the subject, the pace should not be forced. Often those who make slow progress initially, taking time to understand the work, make more rapid progress and show better understanding than children who race ahead at the earlier stages. What is happening is that the latter are quick to perceive techniques although they may not have always grasped the underlying concepts.

AIDING UNDERSTANDING

From the foregoing it should be clear that the aim in giving assistance with mathematics should be to develop overall understanding rather than to give help with a particular problem. This is more difficult to undertake and may not be always successful. One way is to help the child to find out for himself. It may be that you do not understand the problem which is causing him difficulty, so get him to explain it to you. Let him teach you; have him explain it so that you understand it and ask questions until you do. This is a valuable method of approach, since anyone explaining to someone else has to get his ideas clearly sorted out. It may be that in the middle of the explanation your child will suddenly exclaim 'Oh! I know how to do it now'. If not, as you have the problem explained to you, try to work together with your child. In classrooms today, children do not always work in isolation; very often two or three children will work on a problem. This is not 'copying' work from someone else, since each child has a contribution to make and the stimulus of working with others helps development of thought.

It was pointed out earlier that when helping a child, the same language and mathematical methods should be used as he meets at school. Some of the language of mathematics has changed and new words may be used to describe things you knew by another name. Again, ask your child to explain what is meant by that particular word. Also use the index of this book to look up particular terms. Once having learnt the new language, do not forget to use it in discussion with your child.

The same is true of methods. In mathematics there are many different ways of solving a problem and in general you should employ the methods used in your child's school. A well-known example is subtraction, where there are two main methods of setting down the work and finding the answer. Suppose we are doing 62 — 27. As will be explained later, one method is to say 'we reduce the 6 to 5 and take 7 from 12'.

$$\begin{array}{rcc} & {}^{5}\not{6} & {}^{1}2 \\ - & 2 & 7 \\ \hline & 3 & 5 \end{array}$$

In the tens column we then take 2 tens from 5 tens to get the answer 35. The other method takes 7 from 12 as before, but in the tens column increases the 2 to 3, thereby taking thirty from sixty.

$$\begin{array}{rcc} & 6 & {}^{1}2 \\ - & {}^{3}\not{2} & 7 \\ \hline & 3 & 5 \end{array}$$

The answer is 35 as before. It can be imagined what difficulties would be created if one tried to explain the work using one method to a child still struggling to understand the other method.

Nevertheless, provided a child has mastered one method, there are times when encouraging him to find different methods of doing a problem can be a valuable aid to understanding. It is unfortunate that there does not appear to be as much practice as formerly in what used to be called 'mental arithmetic', i.e. working out problems in your head without having to set things down on paper. The two methods of subtraction shown above may not be the easiest way if we are denied the use of paper. Suppose, instead of 62 — 27, we did 62 — 22. Clearly the answer is 40, but we need to take another 5 from this to get the true answer (since 22 is 5 short of 27). So the answer must be 40 — 5 which is 35.

An alternative method would be to find 67 — 27, which is 40, and then say that this answer must be 5 too great since 67 is 5 more than 62. So the answer once more is 35. There are other ways of doing this subtraction problem; can you find some? Experience such as this, where different methods are found to solve the same problem, can be a useful way to encourage mathematical thought.

PROVIDING WIDER EXPERIENCE

It is possible for parents to help all children in their mathematical development, and not just those who are experiencing particular difficulties. The principles set out above apply in all cases and the parent who can help by providing wider experience will be furthering the child's progress.

If we take simple number work as an example, this may be taught in school by the use of a variety of counting apparatus. This may be simple counters, or perhaps the use of fingers, or structural apparatus (i.e. apparatus designed especially for number work, very often consisting of rods or sticks of different lengths; see Chapter 4). But schools use other sources for number work; these may be toys, flowers, plastic shapes and so on. The child is asked to sort these, to add them together, take some away, find how many there are of one colour and how many of another. The teacher talks to the child about these things, asks him to look again if a wrong answer is given, gives a word of praise when the answer is correct, and encourages further investigation.

It is in a similar manner that the parent can help. If it is known what is taking place in school, everyday happenings can be made to yield their share of mathematics. The use of money, household articles, climbing the stairs, flowers in the garden, clocks, going for a walk, the car speedometer and so on, can form suitable starting points for discussion. Some of these have been mentioned already in this chapter, along with games of a mathematical nature. Books of simple puzzles can be a stimulus provided they are suited to the ability level of the child. Even electronic calculators can be a means of stimulating children in their mathematics and providing useful ideas.

Help given to children, whether they are having difficulty or not, should be of a constructive nature aimed to stimulate and encourage. Too often parents fall into an anxiety trap. They may feel that a child is not making progress at a satisfactory rate and go about 'helping' in a way which either creates boredom or produces confusion in the child and does more harm than good. Some parents, for example, express concern if they feel that their child is not doing enough 'sums' in an exercise book and go to the bookshop to buy books with lots of 'sums' in them which become a source of extra practice each evening. Admitted that there may be cases where this is necessary, but if the parent has grasped what has been said in these chapters so far, it will be realized that very often such work is not appropriate. Work with the school; supplement what is being done there in the most appropriate way. Some indications of these ways will be given in the chapters which follow. From these select the topics and the appropriate level of working and understanding.

It must be understood that although topics are covered largely as a whole in what follows, it does not mean that any topic will be covered by the school as one complete set of lessons. It is general practice in schools to do work on a particular topic for some time, then leave it to do work on another topic or a number of topics in succession, returning later to the original topic, revising and doing further work on it before moving on again to other work. In this way, work is constantly revised and extended, and loss of interest, or even boredom, is avoided.

The time to be devoted to the subject must be mentioned. Mathematics is a subject which, on the whole, benefits from being taken in short sessions. It can be a taxing subject for the mind and rest periods are beneficial; by 'rest periods' is meant time away from the subject although other work may go on in those periods. Two half-hours sessions with a break between would probably be more productive than a continuous one-hour session. The time given to the subject in schools and the length of individual sessions varies considerably. A recent survey of time devoted to mathematics in primary schools in England and Wales showed some schools devoting only 30 minutes each day to the subject, whereas other schools had a daily average of 90 minutes for mathematics lessons.

In conclusion, for teachers and parents alike, the key to bringing success to children's study of mathematics comes from creating interest and enjoyment, inspiring self-confidence in the work, and giving a sense of achievement. Parents should bear these points in mind in using what follows to help their children with their work.

4
EARLY WORK

It is necessary to look at the mathematics done in the infant school separately in the first instance, although some of the work covered in later chapters of this book starts in the infant school. The significant feature of infant work is the way in which knowledge is treated largely as a whole. The child is exploring the world about in all its aspects and there is little need to compartmentalize what is learnt, since any piece of knowledge may involve mathematics, science, physical activity, etc. This is good for mathematics (as well as other subjects) since it brings meaning and understanding to the subject. 'I am drinking milk from a carton which is a tetrahedron shape'; 'We found this lovely shell on the sea-shore, look at the spiral'; 'I started in my reading book on page 6, then read page 7 and page 8'; 'In our games lesson we stood around in a circle, then ran to form two straight lines'. In each of these statements there is mathematical language and observation of mathematical properties, but none of them were part of a mathematics 'lesson', nor is the activity described as mathematics.

The first task of an infant teacher is to provide a rich environment within the classroom which can lead to this sort of experience. Naturally these experiences need to be directed along certain lines. A word which is often misunderstood by parents is '*play*'. Children are encouraged to 'play' in the infant school, but what and how they play is carefully contrived by the teacher to lead to certain desired ends; such play is purposeful.

Children may be given plastic shapes and asked to arrange them in patterns, or to 'play' with water and be given a cup, a bottle and a jug to find which holds more. They may be given counters to fit into spaces on a board, thereby matching counters to spaces. Activities such as these provide essential experience upon which basic number work and spatial ideas are built.

The basis of number work lies in children sorting, classifying, matching and ordering materials. *Sorting* is undertaken in a variety of different situations: it may be a case of sorting red flowers and yellow flowers, or plastic motor cars and ships, dolls' clothes or different plastic animals. Sorting leads to *classification* as properties are identified. 'These are elephants; those are horses' is an example, but since many different materials are used, their properties may be used to classify, e.g. large, small, soft, hard, rough, smooth, etc. The result of this work is the arrangement into *sets*: 'This is a set of red objects; that is a set of blue objects.'

The idea of sets is one of the newer aspects of school mathematics. It means exactly what it says: a set of things; a collection. Father has a set of golf clubs; mother uses a set of pans in the kitchen. Once a set has been defined, we can find the number of articles in the set and these are called the *elements* or *members* of the set. The elements of the set of red objects may be a red ball, a red flower and a red pencil-case. Often sets are identified by having a circle, or similar shape, drawn around them.

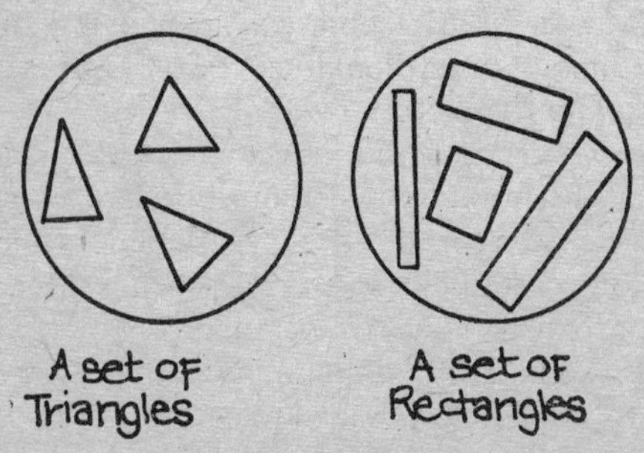

1. **Sets.**

If the set of triangles shown above were combined with the set of rectangles, they would form a set of shapes and there would be seven elements of this new set (3 triangles and 4 rectangles). We speak of this as the *union of sets*. Sometimes, when we are classifying, an object may have properties which fall into more than one category. In the next diagram showing a set of triangles and a set of black shapes, a black triangle clearly lies in both sets and has to be placed as shown.

2. The black triangle is in the intersection of the two sets.

The black triangle is placed in a space known as the *intersection* of the two sets. The opposite process to combining sets is to split a set into a number of *sub-sets*; this is called the *partition* of a set. In the next figure, the set of triangles is partitioned into the set of black triangles and the set of white triangles, each being a sub-set of the original set.

3. The partition of a set.

Returning to the development of work in the infant school, from their activities children are learning language as well as mathematical ideas, and when sorting and playing with shapes, they are developing awareness of space as well as number.

Classification according to properties (e.g. soft, small) leads to *comparison*. Some things are seen to be larger than others; some are heavier than others; some are longer than others. Experiments with young children show that the idea of *equality* is not an easy one for a child to attain, although this fact may seem surprising. Place four spoons (or forks or pencils) well-spaced, beside another four which are more closely spaced, like this:

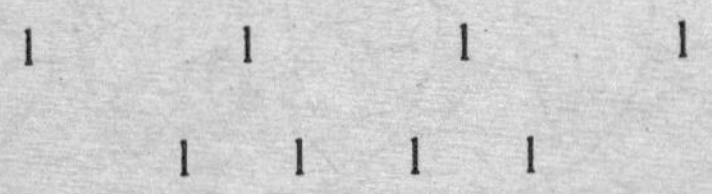

A young child will say that there are more in the first row than in the second, simply because they occupy more space. If the child watches as you move the first row closer together and space out the second row, like this:

| | | |

| | | |

he will then say there are more in the second row than in the first. We say that such a child has not yet achieved the concept of *conservation*. By that is meant the idea that the quantity of material is not altered by the way in which it is arranged.

It should be apparent now that until a child achieves the idea of conservation, he is going to experience difficulty with number work, since he will not recognize, for example, that each of these configurations represents four:

o o   o o o o   o o o
o o   o

Moreover, remembering the earlier statement that concepts cannot be taught, but only acquired through experience, the importance becomes apparent of children handling materials, being encouraged to look at them and to say what they find.

To develop the idea of conservation, the child is engaged in matching things. Teachers often make use of arrow-diagrams for such purposes:

John ⟶ Motor Car
Mary ⟶ Doll
Susan ⟶ Teddy Bear

4. Matching the child with the toy.

In the diagram, the arrow represents that a child has that particular toy. Using the same idea, the elements of one set could be matched onto those of another.

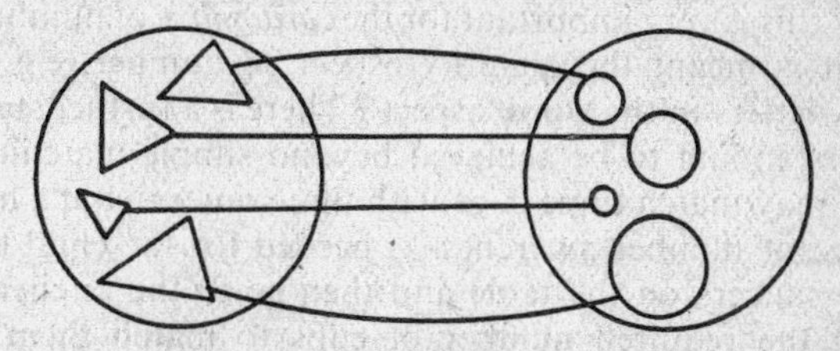

5. Matching the elements of one set on to those of another.

Here a line is drawn connecting each triangle with a circle (sometimes it is said that the triangles have been *mapped* onto the circles). In this instance there is a *one-to-one correspondence* because only one triangle is linked to one circle. In the previous diagram there was also one-to-one correspondence, but it would not be so if, say, Mary had a Teddy Bear as well as a doll.

In Fig. 5, since each element of the set of triangles maps onto an element of the set of circles (do you understand the language?), there must be the same number of triangles as circles. In this diagram:

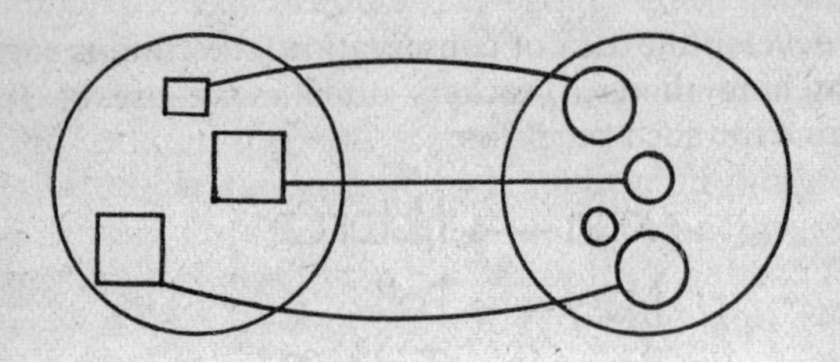

6. The idea of "one more than".

there must be more circles than squares since one of the circles has not been related to a square. Hence the idea of 'one more than ' in the case of the elements of one set compared to those of the other.

All this is very important for the *cardinality* of number, by which is meant the quantity aspect of number, e.g. how many letters in the word 'aspect'? There is a further stage of understanding to be achieved beyond simple matching. A child may match three cups with three saucers, but a higher degree of number awareness is needed for the child to see three saucers on the table and then go to the kitchen and bring the required number of cups to match them. The quantity of three has to be recognized as applied to the cups and saucers; the child perceives three objects, no matter what they are, nor how they are arranged.

In the infant school, work on number is usually graded into stages, the children first handling numbers up to 5. When this work has been understood, they deal with numbers up to 10, then in turn extend this up to 20. There is a surprisingly large amount of knowledge to be learnt about numbers up to 20 and it is essential that this is mastered before going further; for one reason, what takes place with numbers over 20 is largely a repetition of what has been learnt with the first 20 numbers.

As children learn to recognize the quantities which represent the different numbers, they will learn the word and the symbol (e.g. 'three' and '3'). The other aspect of number is the *ordinal* aspect; this is the order of numbers as we count, i.e. first, second, third, fourth, etc. It is important that a child understands the difference between number used in this way and number used in its cardinal aspect. Often a child, asked to bring four pencils from a table, will count them and bring the fourth only; an obvious confusion of cardinality and ordinality. Number experience has to cover both aspects.

There are many aids to a child's understanding of number. One of the most valuable is a number line. This is simply a line with equal spaces numbered along it. It can be used for counting, for adding and subtracting numbers and for many other number operations as will be explained later.

1 2 3 4 5 6 7 8 9 10 11 12 13 14 15 16 17 18 19 20

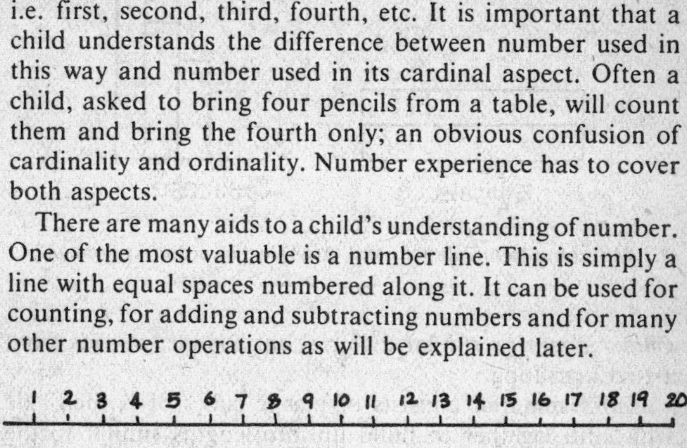

7. A number line.

Children work with sets of objects (e.g. counters, toys, plastic shapes) and recognize the set of 5, the set of 8, etc. They match sets, e.g. they are given a card with a set of 4 dogs drawn on it and have to make up a set of 4 counters to match it.

Another valuable aid at this stage is *structural apparatus*. This is material specially designed to help children with the understanding of number and there are several different types. Probably the best known are Cuisenaire, Unifix and Dienes' apparatus. The last differs somewhat from the other two and will be explained later. *Cuisenaire* consists basically of ten coloured rods of centimetre square cross-section, ranging in length from 1 cm to 10 cm. Children can collect quantities of rods together and match them in length to learn about cardinal numbers or arrange them in order of length to form a 'staircase' (ordinal work) and may add and subtract rods by length as they work on these aspects of number. The diagram illustrates the two activities of matching and arranging in order.

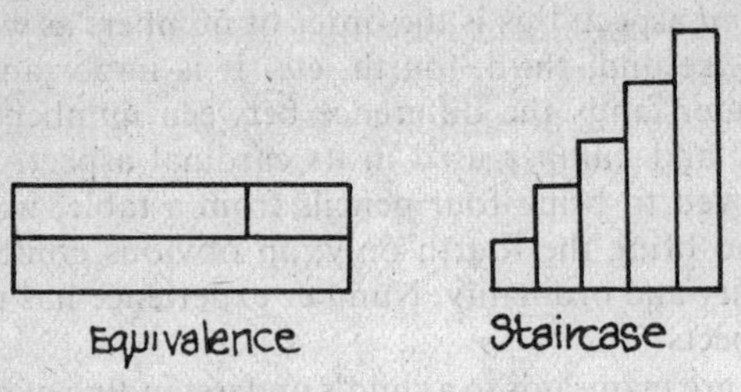

8. Matching (equivalence) and arranging in order (staircase).

Colour Factor is similar material but has twelve rods from 1 to 12 cm long.

Unifix material consists of plastic cubes of ¾ inch side which fit together to build up into lengths similar to the Cuisenaire rods, but whereas the latter are of fixed length, Unifix may be formed to any length and once formed into lengths these may then be split into parts. There is a variety of other material which goes with the Unifix cubes, including trays into which the cubes fit to illustrate such things as the different ways in which numbers may be built up (e.g. $3 = 2 + 1 = 1 + 1 + 1$, etc.), trays with 'staircase' arrangements and also a length of 'number track' into which cubes may be fitted and be used in a manner similar to the use of a number line. There is a similar type of material to Unifix called *Stern* apparatus, but space does not permit either a full list of the different types of structural apparatus or explanations of how it is used. Anyone interested in such material will find manuals are available to explain its use.

The main feature about all structural apparatus is that it concentrates on fundamental mathematical facts and relationships and can be an invaluable tool in number work.

However, it should not be used exclusively. It has been said earlier that the most effective methods make use of many different sources in the building of basic concepts, thus broadening the child's number experience. Many of these sources are simple materials found in the classroom or house. Parents should remember this when they wish to assist their children.

A thorough understanding of number must be attained before a child proceeds to *operations* on number, by which is meant adding numbers, subtracting, and multiplying, etc.

SUGGESTIONS FOR HELP

Nursery rhymes and stories with a number basis, e.g. 'The 3 bears', '1, 2, buckle my shoe'.

Counting materials can be improvised: buttons, coins, lolly-sticks, cocktail sticks, dried peas or beans, etc.

Use everyday situations: cups, saucers, cutlery, petals on flowers. Count the stairs, the number of letters the postman brings, the number of cushions on the chairs, toys, cars parked in a street.

Put things in order, ask for the third, etc. Go to the second drawer. Find the fifth page of the book.

Don't neglect earlier work mentioned above, such as physical characteristics of things being used: soft, heavy, long, etc. Also comparisons: heavier than, bigger than, etc.

Matching: cups and saucers, cushions and chairs, dolls, toys, etc. Toys may be sorted and classified when putting them away: one kind in one drawer, another kind in the cupboard.

THE APPROACH TO ADDITION AND SUBTRACTION

As children are learning the physical properties of numbers, they begin to see the way in which numbers can be made up from other numbers. A set of two buttons and a set of three buttons will form a set of five buttons. Starting with five buttons, it is possible to break up (or partition) the set in various ways: 3 and 2, 4 and 1, 2 and 3, 1 and 1 and 3, etc.

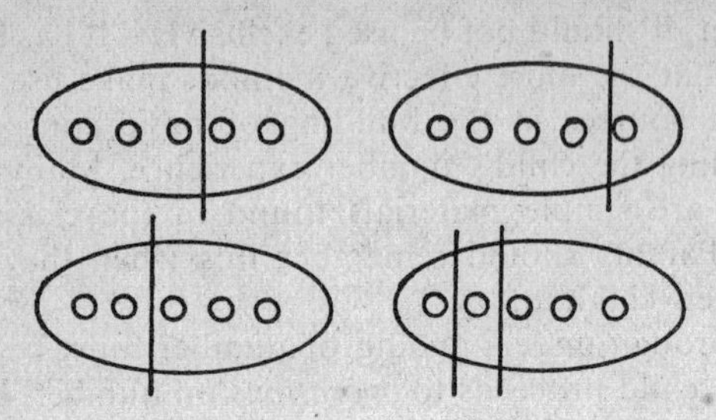

9. Different ways of breaking up a set of five buttons.

So, although the child is initially concerned with appreciating number, the operations – particularly addition and subtraction – begin to enter into the work. A great deal of practice is needed with this composition of numbers up to 10, and especially the way in which 10 can be made up.

Ordinal relationships can be learnt from making 'staircases' with toy bricks, buttons, etc. Different size steps should be used and different starting points employed, e.g. 1, 2, 3, . . . , 10 and 1, 3, 5, 7, 9 and 2, 5, 8, etc.

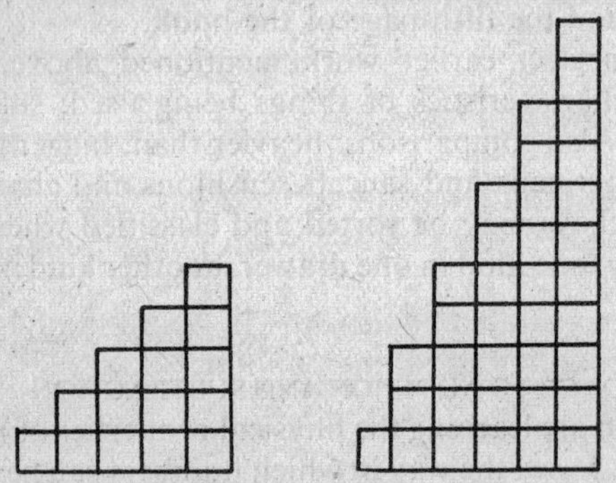

10. Staircases with different size steps.

The value of this work is in the establishment of *number bonds*, i.e. the essential relationships between numbers, such as '5 is 1 more than 4', '3 and 3 make 6', etc. Failure to grasp number bonds leads to subsequent failure in number work. When children are playing with material and combining sets and partitioning sets they are beginning to understand the processes of addition and subtraction. Even when dealing with a staircase such as 2, 4, 6, 8, 10, they are meeting the multiplication tables for the first time. This is why this early work is so important and should not be missed out or rushed. The way in which addition and subtraction are developed in the school will be explained in detail in the next chapter which is concerned particularly with calculation and how it is set down.

Much of the basic work which has been explained above is told by the children in the form of stories, e.g.:

'I had 5 sweets and I gave you 2, so now I have 3.'

'I took 2 bricks and another 2 and I had 4 bricks. I then took 3 bricks and another 1 and I had 4 bricks again.'

Often parents are anxious for children to learn multiplication tables at a very early stage, but this comes later. For the young child, the establishment of number bonds is more important, firstly for numbers up to 10 and then up to 20. Parents can help by asking such questions as:

'What makes up 5?'
'What comes next after 2, 4, 6?'
'Can you count backwards from 8?'
'Count forward in twos starting at 3.'

THE NUMBER LINE AND THE FOUR RULES

The number line was mentioned on page 35 and the processes of addition, subtraction, multiplication and division may be demonstrated by its use. The addition of 4 and 7 is shown by counting off 4, then another 7:

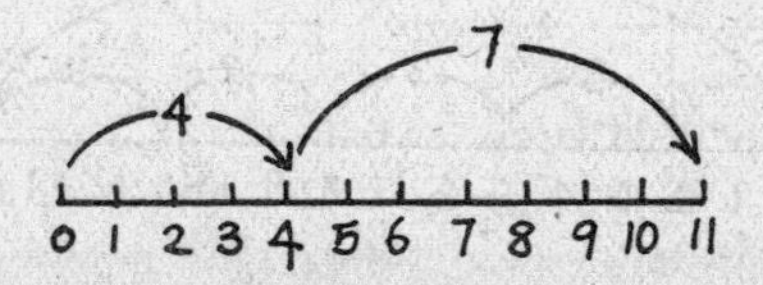

11. Adding four and seven on a number line.

Subtraction of 5 from 9 is shown by first counting off 9 and then counting back a distance of 5.

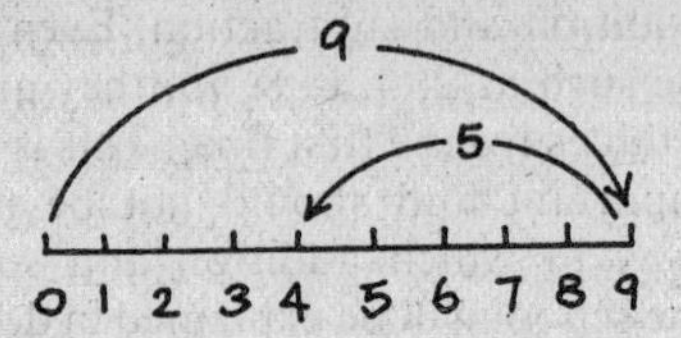

12. Subtraction of five from nine on a number line.

Multiplication is repeated addition, so that 3 × 4 is shown by adding 3 times, a distance corresponding to 4.

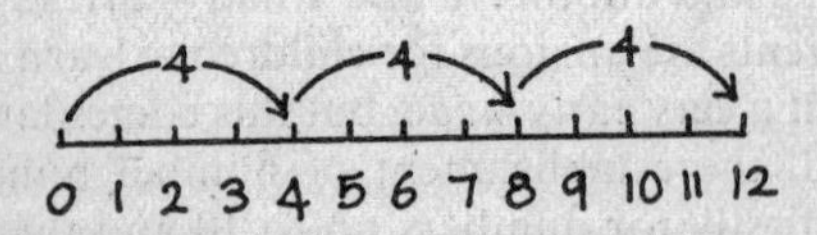

13. Multiplying three by four on a number line.

Finally, division is demonstrated as repeated subtraction. For example, dividing 14 by 3, a distance representing 14 has 3 subtracted from it as many times as possible. The subtraction may take place an exact number of times or (as in this example) there may be a remainder.

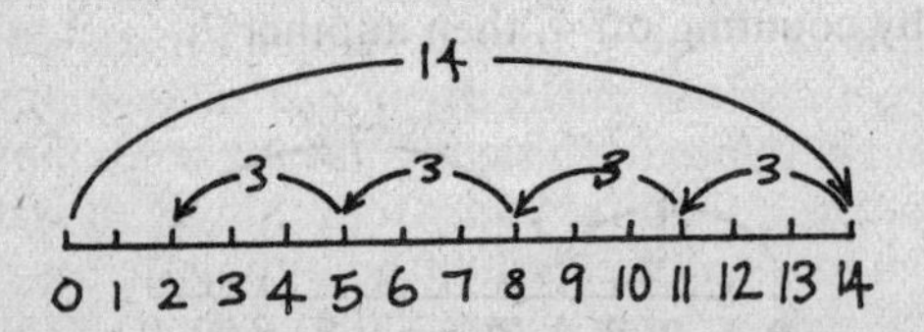

14. Dividing fourteen by three on a number line.

MEASUREMENT AND SHAPES

Mathematics is not concerned solely with calculation and work in the infant school uses the child's experiences for early work on measurement of length, time, weight, area, volume and capacity, appreciation of pattern (i.e. finding relationships) and drawing and recording. Most of these topics are covered in detail later in the book, but it may be useful to indicate the way in which children are given early experience in these aspects of mathematics.

Measurement finds its origins in comparisons: 'longer than', 'heavier than', etc. Children's first measurements are made by using non-standard units such as the span of a hand or a number of strides. Notice the link with number work. At a later stage, the need for standard units becomes apparent because the length of a stride, for example, varies from person to person.

Sand-play and water-play are where the child uses sand or water to fill various containers. The word 'play' is somewhat unfortunate since the work should be directed to definite objectives. The first of these is to help to develop the concept of *conservation*. This was explained earlier in relation to number, but applies equally well in other situations. A child who has not yet achieved the idea of conservation will see a quantity of water in a tall narrow container poured into a wider container and will say there was more water in the first container than there is now in the second; he sees the first container filled to a greater height and makes no compensation for the width. Once again, it is only through experience that understanding is achieved.

Secondly, the filling of containers gives first ideas on volume and capacity, thus developing spatial ideas. Comparison of capacity can lead to numerical relationships when the child develops from saying 'the jug holds more than the cup' to 'I can fill three cups from this jug of water'.

Initial ideas on area arise from fitting shapes together to cover a surface in a tiling pattern. As an example, nine triangles cover the shape below.

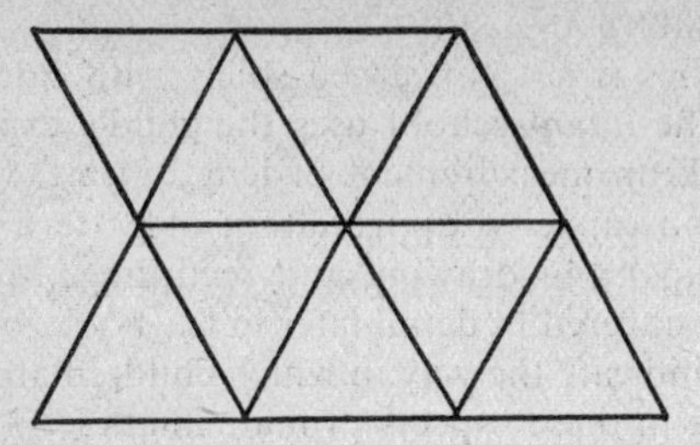

15. Nine triangular tiles.

In addition to an appreciation of size, the recognition and naming of shapes is developed. Once more, observation of real objects forms a basis for the work. In the case of solid objects, the correct names should be learnt – sphere, cylinder, cone, cube, pyramid, tetrahedron, etc. The surfaces are examined: are they flat? are they rounded? will the solids roll? do they slide? Number work can arise from counting the corners or the edges. Children are encouraged to collect containers of different shapes and to make solids out of cardboard.

The same principles apply in the case of plane (i.e. two-dimensional) shapes. Triangles, squares, rectangles, quadrilaterals, parallelograms, pentagons, octagons, hexagons and so on, are handled, named and their properties investigated. The shapes are often made out of coloured plastic or cardboard so that the children may handle them and draw around them.

When shapes are fitted together, a pattern can emerge and children are encouraged to look for these patterns. Pattern indicates some form of *relationship*; relationship lies at the root of mathematics. Patterns can be made by drawing or can be observed in pictures and in wallpapers. There are many opportunities around the home for parents to draw children's attention to pattern.

SUGGESTIONS FOR HELP

These are fairly obvious for this type of work. The danger is that parents do not attach sufficient importance to the place of this work in child development.

Encourage children to collect boxes and containers of interesting shapes, to draw the shapes of the faces, to count corners, edges, etc. Compare different shapes.

Provide opportunities for measuring with water and jugs, cups, bottles, etc.

Have children weigh things in the kitchen. (There is a note about metric and Imperial measures in Chapter 7.)

Cut different shapes from cardboard – triangles, squares, rectangles, etc. – for children to play with. Have them draw around them and cut more shapes from paper. Then fit them together in a tiling pattern or use them to build a solid shape.

Encourage children to collect shells, leaves, stones, etc. of unusual shapes.

Keep old scraps of wallpaper and let the children cut out the shapes and patterns.

Don't forget to discuss with the child; encourage observation; suggest investigations.

REPRESENTATION

As children's mathematical experience develops they begin to write down what they have been doing. Examples were given above of children writing stories about number and they would write similarly about their work with shapes and measurement. They are also doing calculations on paper and the various methods of setting these down are described in the next chapter.

However, there is another way of recording mathematical information which is used extensively – the graph. At the early stages, the work is largely pictorial representation which lies at the heart of graphical work (see Chapter 9).

One type of representation has been used above, where arrows or lines showed the relationship between children and their toys or between the elements of a set of triangles and a set of circles. The graph which displays some statistical information is developed at an early stage. It may be the number of pets (cats, dogs, rabbits, etc.) which the children of the class possess and initially these are represented by paper cut-outs of the animals which are stuck onto a wall-chart as shown below. In the next stage of development, each child sticks a square of paper onto a chart to represent an animal, the columns being restricted to one particular pet.

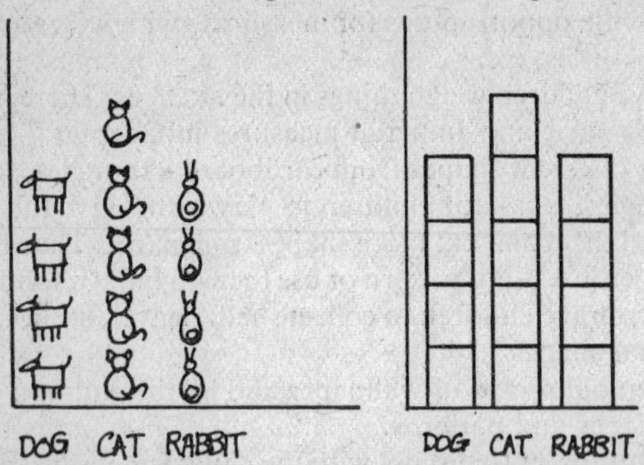

16. Graph showing the number of pets in the class.

At a later stage the children learn to draw columns of appropriate heights to represent the number of each pet owned by the class and we then have the familiar column graphs. Such graphs are constructed for different types of information gathered in class and the work may be linked to other work, e.g. weighing, when a graph is drawn to illustrate the weights of children in the class.

There is no reason why children should not do similar work at home. An example might be recording the days in a month which were sunny, wet or dull, a square being added to the appropriate column each day, or a child could make a graph showing his or her height recorded on the first of each month. Notice that, in school, emphasis is always given to drawing some conclusion from the graph. What does it show? What can we say about it? Once again, we see the importance of discussion with the child.

5
BASIC CALCULATION

Calculation is central to all mathematics. When solving a problem, the mathematician first expresses it in some mathematical form, and then, by calculation, finds a solution to the mathematical expression. If you are buying 5 oranges at 8 pence each, you decide that you can find the cost by working out the mathematical expression 5×8; from this calculation, you know the cost will be 40 pence. Both parts of finding a solution are important: (a) the ability to put the problem into mathematical form, and (b) working out the mathematical expression. In this age of calculators and computers we often use them for (b), but that does not mean that we no longer need to do calculations ourselves. It seems silly to have to use a calculator to work out 5×8, but very valuable to be able to use it for $5{\cdot}8364 \times 8{\cdot}1729$. But, although calculators and computers can be important time-savers, they cannot do part (a) of the problem; we have to think this out ourselves.

Basic calculation, therefore, is an essential part of the mathematical curriculum. Sometimes it is referred to as computation and we talk about children practising *computational skills*; a bit of 'jargon' which really means being able to do calculations. This chapter explains the various ways in which calculation is taught and the ways in which it is recorded (i.e. set down on paper). There are many ways of doing any one calculation and, of course, different ways of teaching it, so alternatives are given. Remember this when helping your child and suit the method to the way he has been taught at school.

ADDITION AND SUBTRACTION OF SIMPLE NUMBERS

Early work on addition and subtraction arises from work with materials. In the previous chapter, the way in which number work was introduced to young children was explained. It was stated that matching of sets takes place by mapping members of one set onto another. If the sets are unequal, the child sees the difference (see Fig. 6, page 34).

When the members of the set of 3 are mapped onto the members of the set of 4, 1 member of the last set is found to be extra. So a set of 4 is 1 more than a set of 3. The use of set ideas is not essential, of course, since similar results can be seen by the use of counters or other material, without using set language.

There are different ways of recording these results. Children may be asked to write '4 is 1 more than 3'. Sometimes exercises are given where an arrow is used to indicate some particular instruction or operation. Often work-cards are made as shown below.

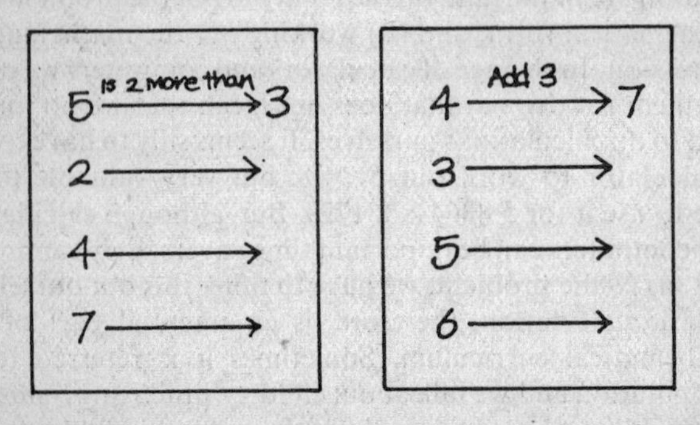

17. Work cards.

Another form of recording is called *box notation*, where a square box is drawn for the child to fill in the missing numbers. (Sometimes mathematical signs are used; sometimes words.)

4 and 3 make □	$6 + 2 = \square$
2 and 5 make □	$4 + 4 = \square$
3 and 2 make □	$7 + 2 = \square$

The box notation is particularly valuable in developing the idea of the relationship of addition and subtraction. An example such as

$$6 + \square = 9$$

is asking the question 'What should be added to 6 to make 9?' This question can be re-phrased: 'How much greater than 6 is 9?' or 'What do you take from 9 to make 6?', thereby introducing the idea of subtraction.

Addition and subtraction are *inverse processes*; subtraction is the inverse of addition and addition is the inverse of subtraction. This means that one process is the opposite of the other; put another way, one process 'undoes' what has been done by the other. If you add 3 and 5 you obtain 8. Now subtract 3 and you are back at 5. Children can see this quite clearly by the use of a number line:

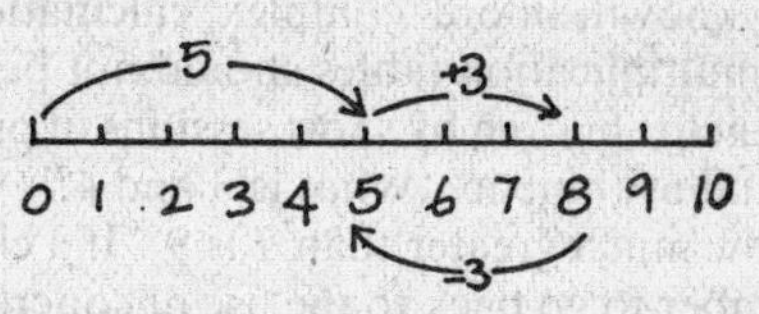

18. A number line shows that addition is the opposite of subtraction.

This idea of inverse processes will be met again later and is extremely important, not only in understanding number work, but in later applications such as in checking work and in finding the solution of equations.

Notice that the word '*subtraction*' has been used; sometimes people talk about 'take away'. However, not all subtractions are 'take away' situations. If I spend £3 and pay the bill with a £5 note, I 'take away' £3 from £5 and find I have £2 change. But there is another aspect of subtraction. If we talk about the difference in the heights of two people, we subtract one height from the other to find the difference, but we are not taking anything away from either person. Both aspects need to be understood and practised and when doing calculations such as 5 — 3 we should talk of subtracting 3 from 5, rather than 'take away'.

In the last chapter, the importance of young children learning number bonds was stressed. In the case of addition and subtraction it is possible to write the same number fact in different forms, e.g.

$$5 + 3 = 8$$
$$3 + 5 = 8$$
$$8 - 3 = 5$$
$$8 - 5 = 3$$

Children should understand this and be able to do the appropriate working with a minimum of effort. Time must be spent mastering these number facts, since until they are thoroughly known, more complex calculations and the learning of multiplication tables should not be undertaken. Parents can help children by short sessions of practice of this type of mental arithmetic. 'What is 3 and 4?' 'What is 2 less than 6?' 'How much greater than 7 is 9?' If a child has difficulty, remember to go back to the use of concrete materials, e.g. counters, sticks, etc., or the number line.

HUNDREDS, TENS AND UNITS

When basic number facts are known, children gradually extend their work into tens, hundreds and so on. In our number system we count in tens and the same *symbol* is used to denote 4 tens as for 4 units. The difference lies in the way we write the numbers, i.e. 44, where the first 4 represents 4 tens and the second 4 represents 4 units. This is known as *place value*, and is simply saying that the value attached to a digit depends on the position in which it is placed. The number 235 really represents 2 hundreds, 3 tens and 5 units (or 200 + 30 + 5). A great deal of difficulty and error is caused by failure to appreciate or remember this.

Children may be introduced to this idea through the use of an abacus. The simplest form consists of vertical spikes onto which rings are dropped. As a total of ten rings is achieved on a spike, they are replaced by one ring on the spike to the left.

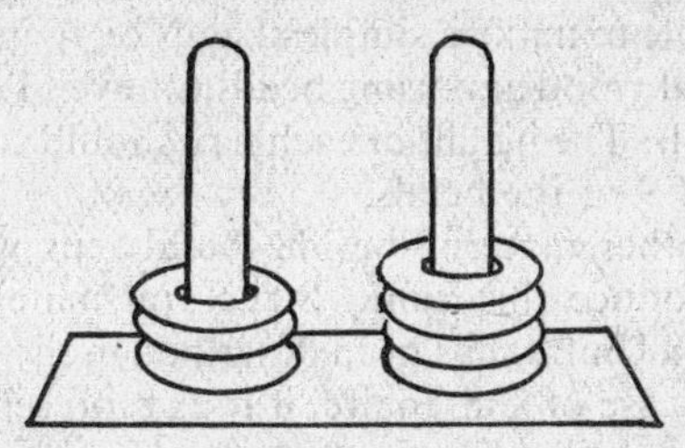

19. The simplest form of abacus.

This corresponds to the way in which children set down a problem:

$$\begin{array}{r} 7 \\ +\ \underline{5} \\ 12 \end{array}$$

The figure carried over to the next column is often set down below that column (this is called a 'crutch' figure) so that it is remembered when the next column is added, e.g.

$$\begin{array}{r} 28 \\ +\ \underline{15} \\ \underline{43} \\ 1 \end{array}$$

Often children doing early work head their columns with H, T or U, as appropriate, to serve as a reminder that digits in those columns represent hundreds, tens or units as the case may be. It is important to stress this, particularly when talking to the child. Look at the last example above. Do you say '5 and 8 is 13; put down 3 and carry 1'? If so, it is incorrect; you are not carrying one over into the next column but ten. It is essential to say 'carry one ten' or simply 'carry ten'. This may seem a small point but it is important to a child's understanding.

It is possible to make a simple abacus by fixing three nails into a piece of wood and using beads (or even Polo mints) to fit on the nails. The height of each nail should correspond to the height of 9 of the beads.

There is other material beside the abacus which can be used to introduce this work. Structural material, such as Cuisenaire or Unifix, has been described in the last chapter. Thus, in the case of Cuisenaire, if rods representing 5 and 7 units are added, then they may be replaced by rods which represent 10 and 2. Similarly with Unifix apparatus; in this case, however, there are also number trays into which columns of Unifix cubes will fit and the unit columns will only take a column of up to 9 cubes, as a reminder that when 10 units are achieved, there has to be a carry-over into the next column.

Another type of apparatus is known as *Dienes' M.A.B.* This consists of small wooden cubes of side 1 cm which represent the *units*. Next there are strips of wood 1 cm square and 10 cm long on which are etched lines to represent cubes, so that it looks like ten unit cubes joined together; these are called *longs*. There are pieces of wood 10 cm square and 1 cm thick with lines marked on them to represent 100 unit cubes; these are called *flats.* Finally there are *blocks* which are cubes of wood of side 10 cm, marked to represent 1000 unit cubes. Numbers may be represented by taking appropriate quantities of each of these; the material is then put together and where there are ten of any particular type (unit, long or flat), they are exchanged for one of the next higher type. The diagram represents the addition of 265 and 157.

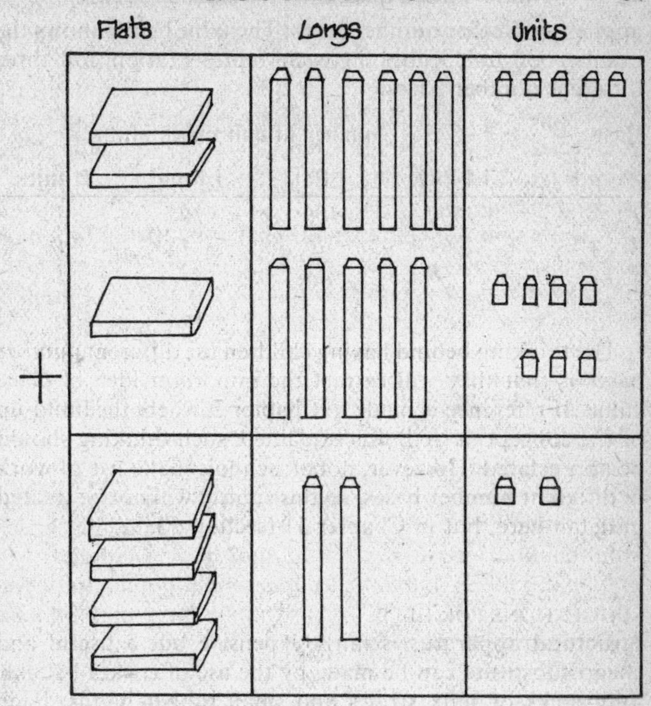

20. Adding with Dienes' M.A.B.

One of the features of Dienes' apparatus is that it is made to serve different *number bases*. We count in tens and this is called the *base* of our number system. But it is possible to count in other bases, for example 8, 3 or 2. To meet this situation, Dienes' material has sets designed for various bases; thus for base 2, the long represents 2 units fastened together, the flat represents 4 units fastened together, and the block 8 units. It will be noticed that, whereas with our tens-system we multiply the number of cubes by 10 each time as we proceed from unit to long, from long to flat and from flat to block, with the base 2 system we multiply by 2. The same applies with other number bases. The table below shows the number of unit cubes in each representation for three different number bases.

Base	Number of unit cubes in:			
	1 block	1 flat	1 long	1 unit
10	*1000*	*100*	*10*	*1*
4	*64*	*16*	*4*	*1*
2	*8*	*4*	*2*	*1*

The thinking behind having children use different number bases is that they will extract the important idea of place value. If reference is made to Chapter 2, where the build-up of the concept of 'red' was explained, such thinking should be appreciated. However, not all schools make use of work in different number bases, so this subject will not be treated in detail here, but in Chapter 11 (section F).

SUGGESTIONS FOR HELP

Structural apparatus is fairly expensive but a useful and cheap substitute can be made by the use of cocktail-sticks, lolly-sticks or milk straws and small rubber bands. Each stick (or straw) represents a unit and these can be made into bundles of ten by using rubber bands. If ten of these bundles are themselves bundled together with another rubber band, they become hundreds. Parents will appreciate the method of use. For example, adding 7 sticks and 8 sticks will produce one bundle of ten and 5 individual sticks, representing 15. Any child having difficulty with the addition of numbers – and particularly 'carrying of figures' – should be allowed to use this material to work out the sum practically. The value of the material in subtraction will be explained below.

Children having difficulty with 'carrying' may find it helpful to write down totals for units and tens additions separately and then do a further addition, e.g.

$$\begin{array}{r} 27 \\ +\underline{68} \\ 15 \\ \underline{80} \\ 95 \end{array} \quad \begin{array}{l} \\ \\ \textit{(from adding units)} \\ \textit{(from adding tens)} \\ \\ \end{array}$$

SUBTRACTION METHODS

Subtraction is a topic which often causes difficulty, is a frequent source of error in children's work and so calls for special consideration. It would seem that many errors arise from methods of recording (i.e. setting the work down on paper) and that many children go through the techniques without really understanding what they are doing. Stress has been placed already on the importance of practical work with material such as counters. Methods of recording should follow the methods of working that have been used with the material, so that understanding of the practical work is transferred to the written work and a child in difficulties can easily return to the practical representation of the problem.

The simplest type of example is where there is straightforward subtraction of units from units, tens from tens and so on, e.g.

$$\begin{array}{r} 75 \\ -\underline{23} \\ 52 \end{array}$$

Difficulties may arise when larger quantities have to be taken from smaller, e.g. in the units column below, where 6 has to be taken from 4.

$$\begin{array}{r} 54 \\ -\underline{36} \end{array}$$

It is important for the child to do this with practical material initially. Suppose that a parent has provided sticks and rubber bands as suggested above, then the child will have 5 bundles of ten sticks and 4 individual sticks. From this he has to take 3 bundles of ten and 6 sticks. This could be written as:

5(10) and 4
3(10) and 6

Since there are only 4 individual sticks and 6 have to be removed, one of the bundles of ten has to be 'un-bundled'. This then gives:

4(10) and 14
3(10) and 6

and subtracting gives:

1(10) and 8

or an answer of 18.

The setting down on paper should follow this method used with the material and may be as follows (where crutches are used):

$$\begin{array}{rrr} & \overset{4}{\not{5}} & {}^{1}4 \\ - & 3 & 6 \\ \hline & 1 & 8 \end{array}$$

This method is known as the *decomposition* method of subtraction. However, another method of subtraction is used in some schools; this is known as *equal additions*.

The difficulty that children may have with the latter method is that they need to appreciate the fact that if one number is being subtracted from another, the result is unaltered by adding the same quantity to each of the two original numbers. As an example, if we know that 35 — 16 = 19, then it follows that 45 — 26 also equals 19, since 10 has been added to both 35 and 16.

Going back to the original problem:

$$\begin{array}{rcr} 54 & & 5(10) \text{ and } 4 \\ & \text{means} & \\ -\underline{36} & & -3(10) \text{ and } 6 \end{array}$$

We now add 10 to the 4 so that we can subtract 6 from 14. This means that the value of the top line is increased to 64, so not only do we have to subtract 6 from that line, but also a further 10. Hence we write:

$$\begin{array}{lrl} & & 5(10) \text{ and } 14 \\ & - & 4(10) \text{ and } \;\;6 \\ \cline{3-3} \text{giving} & & 1(10) \text{ and } \;\;8 \qquad \text{or } 18. \end{array}$$

The corresponding recording which a child has been taught may be as follows (again with crutches):

$$\begin{array}{rcc} & 5 & {}^{1}4 \\ - & \overset{4}{\not{3}} & 6 \\ \hline & 1 & 8 \end{array}$$

If a child is having difficulty with subtraction, take care not to confuse him further by using a method which he does not use at school.

There are, of course, many other ways of doing subtraction, as was pointed out in the last chapter. Using the same example, one could take 30 from 54, giving 24; then subtract 6 from 24, giving the answer 18.

Some of the mistakes which children make in subtraction arise from a failure to appreciate place value, as for example:

$$\begin{array}{rccc} & 6 & 3 & 5 \\ - & 1 & 2 & 8 \\ \hline & & 5 & 7 \end{array}$$

where the fact that there were no tens in the answer has not been recorded with a 0, and the 5 hundreds has been placed in the tens column. Difficulties with taking a larger number from a smaller also account for many mistakes, as in these two examples:

$$\begin{array}{rr} & 172 \\ - & 28 \\ \hline & 154 \end{array} \qquad\qquad \begin{array}{rr} & 172 \\ - & 28 \\ \hline & 156 \end{array}$$

In the first case, the tens adjustment has been forgotten; in the second, the smaller number is subtracted from the larger in each column. Errors need to be looked at carefully. Ask the child to explain what he has done; often the attempt to explain leads him to see the error himself.

The fact that subtraction is the inverse of addition enables a check to be made on answers and children should always be encouraged to check their work. If the number which is being subtracted is *added* to the answer, the result should be the first number, e.g.

$$\left.\begin{array}{r} 172 \\ -\underline{\ \ 28} \\ 144 \end{array}\right\} \quad \text{Add 28 and } 144 = 172$$

MULTIPLICATION

Multiplication first arises as the repeated addition of the same quantity.

For example, 2, 4, 6, 8, 10, . . .
or 3, 6, 9, 12, 15, . . .

Such work is first done when young children are asked to count on (or back) in 2s, 3s, etc. The practical approach by counting objects in rows and columns also forms an early introduction. Arrange a number of pebbles like this:

o o o o o
o o o o o
o o o o o
o o o o o

They could be counted individually, or one could notice that there were five in each row, so that altogether there are $5 + 5 + 5 + 5$, or 4×5.

From facts such as these, the multiplication tables are built up and should be learnt. Usually the order in which the tables are introduced in school is 2, 5, 10, 4, 8, 3, 6, 9, 7. The easy ones are learnt first and the most difficult, the 7 times, is introduced and learnt last. The whole set of multiplication tables can be displayed in one large table:

	1	2	3	4	5	6	7	8	9	10
1	1	2	3	4	5	6	7	8	9	10
2	2	4	6	8	10	12	14	16	18	20
3	3	6	9	12	15	18	21	24	27	30
4	4	8	12	16	20	24	28	32	36	40
5	5	10	15	20	25	30	35	40	45	50
6	6	12	18	24	30	36	42	48	54	60
7	7	14	21	28	35	42	49	56	63	70
8	8	16	24	32	40	48	56	64	72	80
9	9	18	27	36	45	54	63	72	81	90
10	10	20	30	40	50	60	70	80	90	100

The *product* (i.e. the result of multiplying) of any two numbers is obtained by finding one number along the top of the table, the other down the left-hand side, and reading off the number where column and row intersect. There are many other features of this table, some of which are:

1. It may be used to find *factors* of a given number, i.e. numbers which multiplied together equal the given number. Find the given number in the body of the table and read off the corresponding factors down the side and on the top, e.g. factors of 27 are 9 and 3.

2. The numbers in the diagonal which runs from the top left corner to the bottom right are the *square* numbers, 1, 4, 9, 16, etc. These are obtained by mulitplying a number by itself, e.g. $5 \times 5 = 25$ (5×5 can be written 5^2 – read as 'five squared').

3. The numbers in the table are symmetrical about the diagonal containing the squares; notice the way in which the pattern of numbers is the same in both halves of the table. The reason for this is that, for example, $3 \times 4 = 12$ and $4 \times 3 = 12$; similarly for all the other products. We say that multiplication is *commutative*, meaning that it does not matter in which order we perform the operation; if *a* and *b* are numbers, then $a \times b = b \times a$. Addition is also a commutative operation since $a + b = b + a$; e.g. $5 + 2 = 2 + 5$. However, subtraction is *not* cummutative since 5 — 2 does not equal 2 — 5 and similarly for other numbers.

4. The product table may also be used for division of numbers; this will be dealt with in the next section.

The fact that our number system is to base 10 means that the contents of the product table given above are sufficient to enable us to multiply together any two numbers, however large they are. Suppose we wish to multiply two numbers, 27 and 36. We may write:

$$\begin{aligned} 27 \times 36 &= 27 \times (30 + 6) \\ &= 27 \times 30 + 27 \times 6 \\ &= 20 \times 30 + 7 \times 30 + 20 \times 6 + 7 \times 6 \\ &= + 600 + 210 + 120 + 42 \\ &= 972 \end{aligned}$$

Most children will not set the working down in this way, but this method shows clearly the reasoning behind what we do (it makes use of the distributive law as explained in Chapter 11).

Early multiplication work in schools involves multiplying by a single digit number, e.g.

27			27	
× 6			× 6	
42	(from 6 × 7)	*or*	162	(the 4 tens from
120	(from 6 × 20)		4	the 42 are
162				carried as a
				crutch figure)

Having mastered this type of multiplication and setting down of work, children proceed to examples similar to the earlier problem above, perhaps recording it as:

$$\begin{array}{rl} 27 & \\ \times\ \underline{36} & \\ 162 & \text{(from } 27\times 6) \\ \underline{810} & \text{(from } 27\times 30) \\ 972 & \end{array}$$

Some may multiply 27 by 30 first so that the third and fourth lines of the working above would be interchanged. Returning to the original explanation, it will be seen that this does not make any difference, since they have expressed $27 \times (30 + 6)$ as $27\times(6+30)$ and from the commutative property of addition, we know that $30 + 6$ is the same as $6 + 30$.

Children need to practice multiplication, particularly arising from real situations. Money calculations (e.g. the cost of 18 articles at 34 pence each) and area (see Chapter 7) are two obvious applications. The more often calculation processes are seen in different circumstances, the better will be the understanding of their use.

DIVISION

Just as subtraction has two aspects – 'take away' and 'difference between' – so does division arise in two ways. It is essential that children experience and appreciate both of these. Suppose I wish to share £40 between four boys, then, dividing 40 by 4, I find that each boy will receive £10. Next suppose I have a tank containing 40 litres of water; how many times can I fill a 4 litre can from this tank? Again I divide 40 by 4 and obtain an answer of 10 times.

However, the two problems are very different. In the first example, the money is being shared out equally. A diagram may make this clear, starting with a set of 40 £1 notes and re-distributing into 4 sets of 10 £1 notes each – in the manner of dealing 4 hands at cards.

Since the process is one of sharing equally,

(i) each boy must receive the same amount,
(ii) *all* the original money must be distributed.

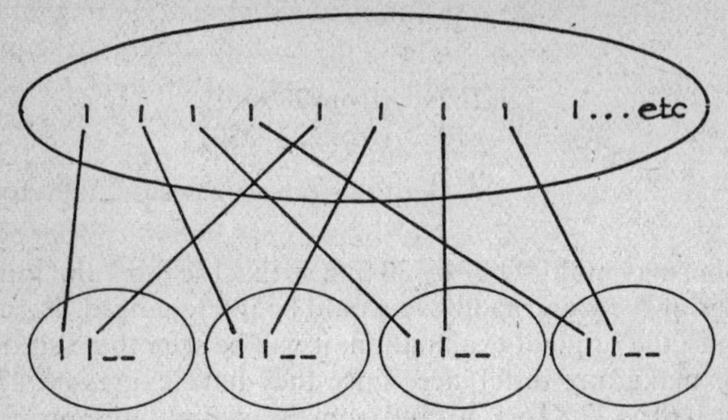

21. **Dividing up in the manner of dealing four hands at cards.**

If, for example, there had been £41 originally, then it would be necessary to share the extra £1 equally among the four boys; each would then receive £10.25.

In the second example, nothing is being shared. Instead 4 litres of water is being taken repeatedly from the water in the tank. Representing this in a diagram, the process is one of breaking up the original set into ten sub-sets, each of 4 litres.

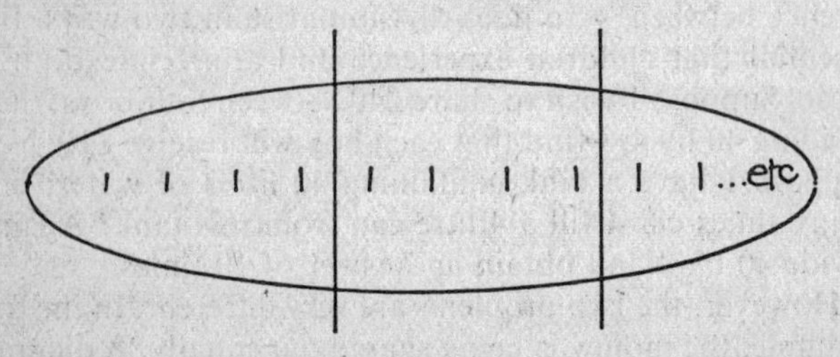

22. **Breaking a set up into sub-sets.**

This process of 'breaking up' a set into sub-sets is called partitioning, so that this aspect of division is sometimes called the *partitive* aspect. If we do not use set language, it could be called repeated subtraction because a certain amount is being subtracted from the original each time. The important difference between this type of division and the sharing process described above is that if there had been 41 litres of water in the tank, the can could have been filled 10 times and there would have been one litre of water left in the tank. This would be a remainder. With this type of division, therefore, we may have a remainder, whereas with the sharing process there can be no remainder and fractional parts may appear in the answer.

Children doing early work on division start with practical examples, e.g. a pile of counters or buttons has to be shared out equally between a number of people; how many times can equal lengths be cut off from a given strip of paper? Initially the work does not involve fractions or remainders and checking the final results will lead to an appreciation of the fact that division is the *inverse* process of multiplication. For example, if 20 pennies are shared between 4 people, each receives 5 pence. Now that 4 people each have 5 pence, find the total; clearly this is $4 \times 5 = 20$ pence.

Since multiplication and division are inverses, the product table given in the section on multiplication may be used to do simple division. If 12 has to be divided by 4, find 4 down the left-hand side of the table, read the numbers along this row until 12 is found, then find the number at the top of the column in which 12 lies; in this case 3.

There are certain terms connected with division. The working $12 \div 4 = 3$ may be used as an illustration. The number which is to be divided (12 in this case) is called the *dividend*; the number by which it is to be divided is called the *divisor* (4 in the example); the result of the division (3) is called the *quotient*.

There are various ways in which the working of division calculations is set down. Initially problems will involve division by single figure numbers only. A method of recording is shown below which gives particular emphasis to the value of numbers in the quotient as they appear, but it should be stressed once more that the method to be followed with a child should be that taught in the particular school.

```
          4        20+4=24
         20
    4 ) 96
        80
        16
        16
         0
```

The emphasis in the above working is on the fact that when 90 is being divided by 4, the answer is 20, and not 2, as is frequently the case when the child says '4 into 9 goes 2 times'. The snag with this method, of course, is that the answer does not emerge as 24, but as two separate quantities, 20 and 4. A child who is told to do it in this manner after having used a different method, could quite easily write down the answer as 204.

Division, in fact, is a difficult topic and only comes second to subtraction as a source of children's mistakes with calculation. It is particularly important, therefore, that children should be taught to check their answers. Since division is the inverse of multiplication, the answer to a division problem should be multiplied by the divisor to see that the result is the same as the dividend. To check the example above, multiply the answer, 24, by 4 to obtain 96. Further development of the idea of inverses appears in Chapter 11 (section E).

SUGGESTIONS FOR HELP

It was pointed out earlier that $4+3=7$, $3+4=7$, $7-4=3$ and $7-3=4$, all embody the same number fact. Similarly, in the case of multiplication and division, examples such as:

$$3 \times 4 = 12$$
$$4 \times 3 = 12$$
$$12 \div 3 = 4$$
$$12 \div 4 = 3$$

are different forms of the same number relationship. Hence when multiplication tables are being learnt and practised, the division relations should be practised too. Questions such as 'What are three fours?' should be interspersed with questions like 'What number multiplied by 4 makes 12?' and 'What is 12 divided by 3?'

Parents will wish to give the children practice examples to do. An important point to remember is that these should be graded, with simple ones first. If parents wish to make up examples, they should ensure that a full range of practice is given, although additional emphasis will be given to known weaknesses, e.g. a particular multiplication table. Also, remember not to overdo this work; short sessions are essential and the work should be enjoyable and interesting.

APPROXIMATING AND CHECKING

It has been stressed that checking of results should take place whenever possible. This is true of all mathematical work; errors can creep in and lead to wrong answers.

Methods of checking calculations vary considerably and it is for each individual to devise suitable means. With simple calculations, however, the most important check is to ask 'Is the answer reasonable?' In practical problems we should have some idea of what to expect: what are reasonable quantities? Does this length, or weight, or speed seem correct? We shall return to this point in Chapter 7 when measurement is considered.

But we should also be able to say what the approximate result of any calculation will be. This is done by taking simple numbers which approximate to the actual figures and doing an easy calculation to give an answer which should roughly equal the actual result. We start by what is known as *rounding* of the figures in a calculation; this means taking them to the nearest ten or nearest hundred, etc. Thus for 38 we would round to 40, whereas for 72 we would round to 70, since 38 is nearer 40 than to 30 and 72 is nearer to 70 than to 80. With a number such as 369, we would round it to 400. In the case of a number such as 650, which is half-way between 600 and 700, we round up to 700.

These approximations enable us to perform a simple calculation which will indicate what the true answer should be. Thus when multiplying 57 and 42, they are rounded to 60 and 40 and multiplied to obtain an answer of 2400. The true answer is 2394, which agrees with the rough estimate. An answer close to the estimate may still be wrong, but it seems more likely to be correct than one which differs widely from the estimate. The basis of this type of rough check is, of course, the ability to perform simple calculations, such as 60×40, quickly; an emphasis of the point made earlier that 'mental arithmetic' still has a place in mathematical education.

There are other ways in which calculations can be checked, mainly by doing further calculation. The weakest check is to repeat the calculation, since any error is quite likely to be repeated. The best checks are either to do the calculation by some other method, or to start with the answer which has been obtained and work back to the start of the problem.

Children should be encouraged to check their working at all times. Unfortunately this is not always stressed in schools, and children, faced with a number of examples to do, are only too anxious to get an answer and carry on with the next example.

THE LANGUAGE OF MATHEMATICS

From the earliest stages of education, as children learn mathematics, they are also extending their vocabulary. As with all language, there is usually more than one way of expressing an idea in mathematics and children should meet and understand these different words and be able to use them correctly.

To illustrate what is meant, here are some of the different ways in which one may be asked to add two numbers, 3 and 4:

Add 3 and 4.
What is 3 plus 4?
What is the sum of 3 and 4?
Given the numbers 3 and 4, find their total.

There are four words here – add, plus, sum, total – which describe the same operation of addition.

The same could be said of other operations, e.g. times, multiply, product, all describe the process of multiplication. Unless children become familiar with these words, they will fail in their mathematics, not because they do not know what to do, but because they do not know what they are being asked to do. Subtraction and division create special difficulties since the numbers do not have to be in the same order. Thus we may say 'From 43 subtract 28' or 'Subtract 28 from 43'; children setting this down in vertical form often write the first number above the second, like this:

$$\begin{array}{r} 43 \\ -\underline{28} \end{array} \quad \text{and} \quad \begin{array}{r} 28 \\ -\underline{43} \end{array}$$

with consequent difficulties in the second case.

There is a need, therefore, for children to talk about their mathematics so that they become familiar with the language. To some extent this is provided for in the modern classroom where children are encouraged to work together and to discuss their work with other children and with their teacher. This can be continued at home when children are doing work with a mathematical content. Carefully chosen questions from a parent can encourage them to say what they are doing and why, thereby clarifying their own thoughts and giving them practice in the use of vocabulary.

EXTENSION OF THE NUMBER SYSTEM

So far we have dealt with simple calculations involving whole numbers which arise from counting and measuring. These are the numbers

$$1, 2, 3, 4, 5, 6, 7, 8, 9, 10, 11, \ldots$$

which we call counting numbers, or more usually, the *natural numbers.* If we are thinking in terms of sets, the set of natural numbers is interesting because there are an infinite number of members of the set. In other words, we can go on counting in the same way for ever, the numbers getting larger and larger. We speak of an *infinite set* in such cases, in contrast to a set of four numbers only – 2, 4, 6, 8, say – which make up a *finite set*. A finite set is one where there is a limited number of members of the set.

In this chapter we have considered the four basic operations on number: addition, subtraction, multiplication and division. Firstly, consider the addition of any numbers from the set of natural numbers, e.g. 5 and 8. Adding these we obtain 13, which is a member of the set of natural numbers. This is true, whatever two numbers are chosen; in other words, adding two natural numbers results in a natural number. Hence the operation of addition can take place within the set of natural numbers. When this is true, we say that we have *closure* for that operation.

Now consider subtraction. Once more, take two natural numbers, 4 and 9 say. Take 4 from 9, the answer is 5, which is a natural number but if we take 9 from 4, there is no answer in the set of natural numbers. In order to obtain an answer to problems such as $4 - 9$ we have to extend the number system to include negative numbers. This new set of numbers is:

$$\ldots -4, -3, -2, -1, 0, 1, 2, 3, 4, 5, 6, \ldots$$

(where the dots before and after the numbers indicate that the numbers continue in that way to infinity).

These numbers are called the *integers*, or to be more precise, they are the set of positive and negative integers with zero. Using this set of numbers it is possible to perform any subtraction and obtain an answer within the set. Thus $4 - 9 = -5$. In other words, there is now closure for subtraction.

Next turn to multiplication. In the set of natural numbers, is there closure for multiplication? The answer is yes, since taking any two numbers (e.g. 3 and 4) and multiplying them, the answer is always a natural number.

However, division is not closed, since a problem such as

$3 \div 5$ can not have an answer which is a natural number. Once more the number system has to be extended, this time by including *fractional* numbers. These may be either *vulgar fractions* ($\frac{3}{5}$ in the case of $3 \div 5$) or *decimal fractions* (0·6 in the case of $3 \div 5$). Notice that people very often speak of fractions (meaning numbers such as $\frac{3}{8}$) and decimals (meaning numbers such as 0·3), but strictly speaking, both are fractions, the word fraction meaning a part of something.

So finally there is a set of numbers which includes the positive and negative integers and fractions together with zero, in which we can obtain answers to any problem involving the four operations of addition, subtraction, multiplication and division. This is called the set of *rational numbers*. Operations within these new sets of numbers need further consideration. Fractional numbers will be considered separately in Chapter 6 and negative numbers are dealt with later in this chapter. Nought or zero is discussed in Chapter 11.

Before leaving the matter of different types of numbers, however, it should be pointed out that there are other types which have not been mentioned above. One such set of numbers is the *irrational numbers*. These may be explained as numbers which cannot be measured exactly. The rational numbers which have been dealt with so far, can all be measured exactly, e.g. $1\frac{3}{4}$ metres. We can also measure negative quantities, e.g. — 5° on a thermometer. Not so the irrational numbers.

If a number is multiplied by itself, it is said to be squared, e.g. 3×3, which is written as 3^2. Clearly $3^2 = 9$. If we reverse the process, we are finding the square root. Three squared is nine, so the square root of nine is three. Or in symbols:

$$3^2 = 9, \text{ so } \sqrt{9} = 3.$$

Similarly $\sqrt{16} = 4$, $\sqrt{25} = 5$ and so on. But what about $\sqrt{5}$ or $\sqrt{7}$? The square root of 4 is 2 and the square root of 9 is 3, so the square root of 5 must lie between 2 and 3. But it cannot be worked out exactly. The first eight figures for the square root of 5 are 2·2360679, but if you square this number you obtain a number which is slightly less than 5. The same would be true for the square root of 5 to eighty figures or to eight hundred figures; square the result and the answer would be slightly less than 5. Numbers such as this, whose value cannot be determined exactly, are called irrational numbers. Another example is the number of times that the circumference of a circle is greater than its diameter. This number is denoted by π (the Greek letter 'pi'). An approximate value of π is 3·1415926, but computers have produced better approximations which have many thousands of decimal places.

Another type of number which primary children are likely to meet is a *prime number*. This is a number, other than 1, which will only divide by itself and 1. Thus 7 is a prime number, since its only factors are 7 and 1. But 8 is not prime, since it can be divided by 8, 4, 2 and 1. Notice that 1 is not a prime number; the first eight prime numbers are 2, 3, 5, 7, 11, 13, 17 and 19.

NEGATIVE NUMBERS

It is proposed to consider here the four rules as applied to negative numbers. Not all primary schools will cover this work; most will probably mention negative numbers, some will deal with their addition and subtraction, but not many will cover their multiplication and division.

The idea of a negative number is best illustrated by extending the number line backwards. We have earlier used a number line for positive numbers and counting backwards gives the following:

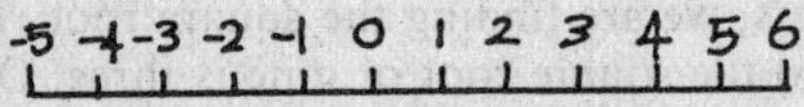

-5 -4 -3 -2 -1 0 1 2 3 4 5 6

23. Extending the number line backwards.

The idea of negative numbers is of fairly frequent occurrence and an example is to be found with temperature. We are now accustomed to the idea of negative temperatures in such instances as home freezers which should be maintained at a temperature of —18°C or below. Thermometers for use in such cases have a scale extending both ways from 0° in a manner similar to the number line above.

One difficulty arises with regard to negative numbers. Look at the two signs here:

$$8 - 3$$
$$-18°\text{C}$$

In the first case, the minus sign indicates an operation, i.e. it is telling you to do something, in this case subtract 3 from 8. In the second case, the minus sign is indicating a certain state or position on a scale. The two are entirely different, yet the same sign is used, —, and the same word, minus, to indicate both. This can be confusing and of late some teachers of mathematics have tended to separate the two. Where the process of subtraction is indicated, the normal sign is used, e.g. 8 — 3. Where the state or position is shown, the sign is raised slightly, e.g. $^{-}6$ and is called 'negative six', *not* 'minus six'. So in the case where we are subtracting $^{-}6$ from a number, we would write it as $8 - {}^{-}6$ and read it as '8 minus negative 6'. This scheme of notation does assist understanding and explanation of the work involving negative numbers and will be used in the work which follows. The one snag is that in science and in everyday life we do not say 'negative 18 degrees' but 'minus eighteen degrees'. Remember, too, that if a child is not familiar with this notation in his school work, it may be better not to introduce it, but to use the methods which he has been taught.

Addition involving negative numbers is straightforward if one uses the number line. $3 + 2 = 5$ is easily seen, and the working of an example such as $^{-}2 + 6$ is exactly the same, giving an answer of 4.

Notice that a negative number is counted from right to left, so in the second diagram below, $^{-}2$ is measured from 0 to the left, after which 6 is added. If two negative numbers are being added, e.g. $^{-}3 + {}^{-}2$, we start by counting $^{-}3$ to the

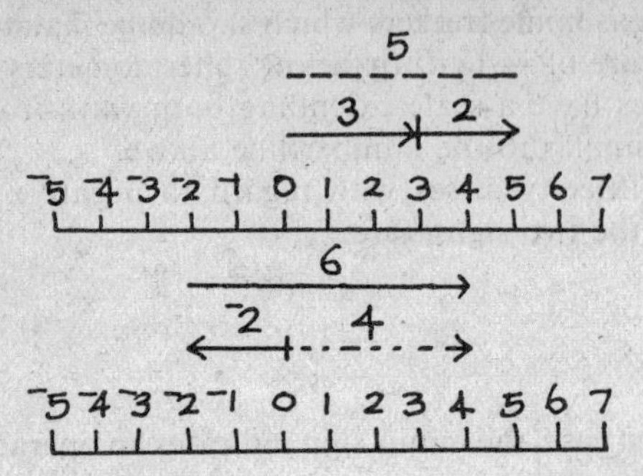

24. Adding a negative number to a positive number in a number line.

left of zero, then add a further ⁻2 in the same direction, giving an answer of ⁻5.

25. Adding two negative numbers on a number line.

Subtraction of negative numbers is best explained by use of the box notation used earlier in this chapter. To work out 7 — 4, it would be written 7 — 4 = □. This may be expressed in a different form by asking what must be added to 4 to obtain 7, or 4 + □ = 7. Drawing a diagram for the problem, the answer is seen to be 3:

26. Subtracting a positive number on a number line.

Now take the example $7 - {}^{-}3 = \square$ where ${}^{-}3$ is being subtracted from 7. Re-writing this as in the last example:

$${}^{-}3 + \square = 7$$

(or 'what must be added to ${}^{-}3$ to obtain 7?'). The diagram below shows that the answer is 10.

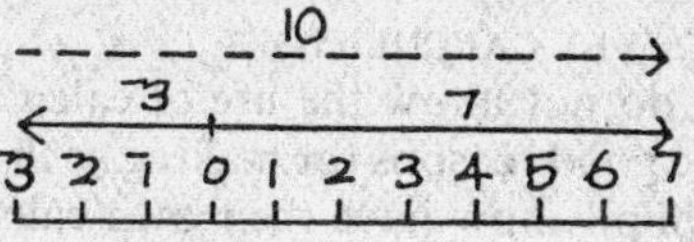

27. Subtracting a negative number on a number line.

So the problem and its answer may be written

$$7 - {}^{-}3 = 10.$$

Since $7 + 3$ is 10, subtracting ${}^{-}3$ was the same as adding 3. The same is true of other numbers, of course, e.g. $5 - {}^{-}4 = 9$. A rule becomes established and is soon learnt: subtracting a negative number is the same as adding that (positive) number.

Once the rule is learnt, many people forget the reason for it and cannot explain why it should be so.

Multiplication involving negative numbers is best explained by making use of the fact that multiplication is repeated addition. There are three different cases:

(a) $4 \times 3 = 12$ is really $4 + 4 + 4 = 12$
So ${}^{-}4 \times 3$ is ${}^{-}4 + {}^{-}4 + {}^{-}4 = {}^{-}12$

(b) Subtracting 1 from zero on the number line gives ${}^{-}1$
Doing this four times, ${}^{-}4$ is equivalent to $-1 - 1 - 1 - 1$
So $3 \times {}^{-}4 = -3 - 3 - 3 - 3$ which gives ${}^{-}12$

(c) Similarly, ${}^{-}3 \times {}^{-}4$ is equivalent to

$$- {}^{-}3 - {}^{-}3 - {}^{-}3 - {}^{-}3$$

and from the rule established above, this equals

$$3 + 3 + 3 + 3$$

Hence ${}^{-}3 \times {}^{-}4 = 12$

The rules for signs in division may be obtained by regarding division as the inverse of multiplication. However, as stated earlier, few primary schools will be doing work involving multiplication and division of negative numbers and the outline above is given mainly for completeness and as background for parents to refer to should the need arise.

THE USE OF POCKET CALCULATORS

Some schools do not allow the use of calculators by their pupils and give good reasons for making such a rule. Nevertheless many pupils now have their own calculators and it seems a pity to say that they should not use them. Calculators are here to stay and it seems appropriate to try to make use of them in a positive way in a child's education. It would be stupid to suggest that children who have a calculator need no longer do any calculation without its use. Practice in basic calculation, such as the work covered in this chapter, is essential both for an understanding of the different types of calculation and also the ability to perform simple calculations quickly and to make checks of more complex workings which may have been done by calculators.

Where the calculator comes into its own is in dealing quickly with complex calculations and those involving awkward numbers. We do not need a calculator to work out 7×8, but there is a saving of time to use it to find $7{\cdot}8356 \times 8{\cdot}2614$. In fact, the arrival of the pocket calculator would seem to have the effect of re-emphasizing the ability to perform simple calculations in one's head.

Children enjoy playing with a pocket calculator and there is no reason why it should not be used to develop calculating abilities. Problems on the four rules can be set for the child to work out manually, then answers obtained can be checked by use of the calculator.

Another method of use is in the learning of multiplication tables. Most calculators will retain a number as a constant multiplier. That is to say, you can enter a number such as 7, and multiply a succession of numbers by 7, simply by entering those numbers in turn. Calculators work in different ways, so the instruction leaflet may have to be consulted. However many of them operate as follows for a constant multiplier:

Enter 7 in calculator.
Press × key.
Enter 5.
Press = key. This should give an answer of 35.
Enter 6.
Press = key. This should give an answer of 42.

You may then continue to find 7 × any number by entering that number, followed by pressing the = key. (If the calculator does not work in this manner, either experiment or see the instruction leaflet.)

To apply this to the learning of tables, suppose a child wishes to test himself on the 7 times table. He proceeds as above to put 7 as the constant multiplier. He now says aloud 'Seven eights are . . . .' (whatever he believes the answer to be). He then puts 8 into the calculator, presses the = key and can see whether he was correct. He can repeat for other multiples of 7. In a similar way, other tables can be tested.

Particular calculations or puzzles performed on the calculator can stimulate children's mathematical interest and thought. Here is an example. The numbers on a calculator keyboard are arranged as follows:

7 8 9
4 5 6
1 2 3

Enter any three-figure number which you can see in a straight line passing through 5, e.g. 753, 159, 654, etc. Now add this number reversed, e.g. 753 + 357 = . The answer is always 1110; why is this?

FACILITY IN CALCULATION

The ease with which problems, particularly calculations, are done is something which really cannot be taught. It can be encouraged, it arises from an interest in mathematics, from a keenness to meet the challenge of a problem and from earlier experience in problem solving. To illustrate the point, consider the following problems:

(a) Work out 256 × 8
(b) Work out 512 × 4

In both cases the answer is 2048. Having found the answer to (a) by multiplication, there is no need to do a multiplication in (b) since 256 is doubled to obtain 512 and 8 is halved to obtain 4, so the answer will be the same. It is the ability to see such situations and to choose the most economical methods of working, that we are speaking of, when we refer to a child's facility in calculation. If the child does not see the connection between (a) and (b) and does the multiplication in problem (b), we can explain it to him and follow with example (c) or (d):

(c) Work out 128 × 16
(d) Work out 64 × 32

Probably he now sees an easier way to do these problems and thereby finds the answers, but we have only taught him one particular technique. Ask him to do problem (e):
(e) A man is paid 9½ pence per kilometre to run his car. How much is he paid when he travels 400 kilometres?

Once more there is an easy way to do the problem. 400 tenpences are 4000 pence or £40. But we must deduct 400 halfpence, i.e. 200 pence or £2. So the man is paid £38. This is much easier than multiplying 400 by 9½. But does the child use such a simpler method? The technique shown in (a) and (b) does not help in any way, except for illustrating the general idea that one should think carefully about the methods to be used for solving a problem and try to select the best. This may often involve finding one's own methods.

An 11-year-old boy had written this in his exercise book:

	243
~~1100~~	572
160	314
	144
	12

When asked what he was doing, he said it was a problem about distances which involved adding 243, 572, 314 and 144. 'But what are you writing down?' he was asked. 'Well,' said he,'I add 2 hundreds, 5 hundreds, 3 hundreds and 1 hundred and I get 1 thousand 1 hundred which I write at the side. I then add up the tens and they come to 160 and I write this at the side. I already have 1100 and I have another hundred from the 160, so I have 1200 and I put 1 in the thousands column of the answer and 2 in the hundreds column. Next I am going to add the units; they come to 13. I add the ten to the sixty I have got already and my answer will be 1273.'

Notice that, whereas normally in written addition problems, the units are added first, then tens and so on, he had reversed the process and started by adding the hundreds. There is nothing wrong with this method, of course, but curious to know why he did it this way, he was then asked who had taught him this method. 'No one,' he replied, 'I couldn't understand the way I was shown at school, so I went home and invented this method for myself!'

The point about the story, which is true, is that the boy had gone about solving the problem in his own way; he had found his own method of solution, thereby showing that he understood the principles. It does not follow that he would continue to use this method; at a later stage he might change to a different method which he considered to be more effective. It is interesting to note that the method he used is that used by people who can perform complicated addition problems mentally. If you try to add the four numbers mentally, starting with the units, you may have difficulty in remembering parts of the answer; next try it by adding the hundreds first and you will find that this method is much easier.

A child can be encouraged to think about mathematical problems and look for better methods of solution, by the approach which is adopted in many schools, of getting children to do the same problem in a variety of ways. On the other hand, some schools are opposed to such methods, saying that they lead to confusion in the child's mind and uncertainty about how to do calculations. Probably in the latter cases, the attempt is being made to *teach* the child the different techniques, possibly also at a time when he has not learnt thoroughly the basic processes outlined in this chapter. The method is one of encouragement of the child to seek an appropriate method of solution; if he comes up with more than one method, ask which he considers to be the better way and why. If he can only find one method of solution, do not pursue the matter further – you cannot do the thinking for the child.

6
FRACTIONS, DECIMALS AND PERCENTAGES

In the last chapter it was explained how the idea of fractional parts of a whole can be developed as part of the number system, but children's introduction to the idea of fractions comes from reference to practical situations. The child sees many examples of halves and quarters in everyday life; these are the commonest fractions. At the infant stage, therefore, children are given further experience with these fractions. Plastic shapes are fitted together, paper is folded and cut, structural apparatus is used in certain ways and children discuss the parts of the whole that they discover there. The diagram below shows some ways in which this is done; a square divided into four quarters, a length of material with a quarter marked off, a circle or a round cake with a quarter removed, a set of cubes with a quarter indicated by colour, and the face of a clock with the minute hand covering a quarter of an hour.

In number work, fractions arise from relationships, often from inverses of multiplication. For example, a child may say 'I have six pennies and you have three pennies. I have twice as many pennies as you and you have half as many pennies as I.' Another example would be: 'There are two counters in this set and eight counters in that set, so this set has a quarter of the counters of that set and that set has four times as many counters as this set.' Or the idea may be developed as part of the work on the partitioning of sets. The diagram shows $\frac{1}{4}$.

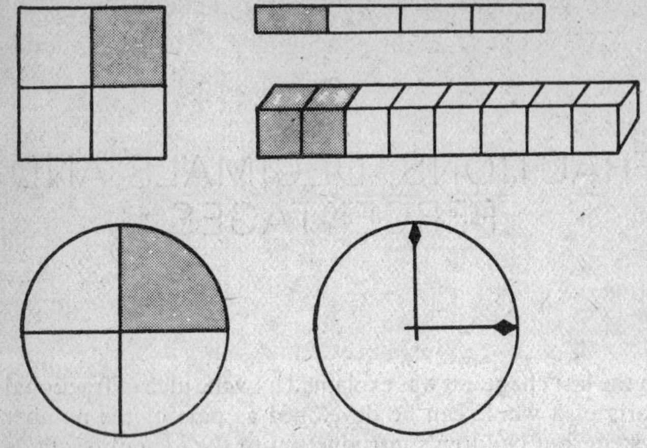

28. Different ways of showing a quarter.

The idea that two fractions make up a whole (e.g. $\frac{3}{4}$ and $\frac{1}{4}$) develops with the understanding that the denominator (in this case, 4) represents the total number of parts and the numerator (3 or 1 here) represents the number of parts taken.

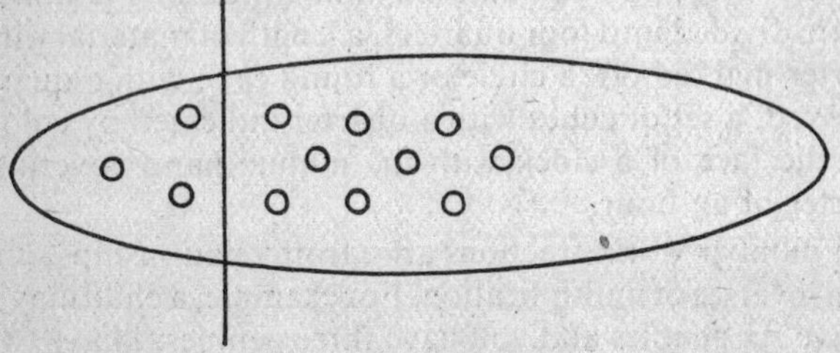

29. Partitioning of a set to show a quarter.

EQUIVALENCE OF FRACTIONS

Although quarters and halves are the commonest fractions, experience with materials, or by partitioning sets, introduces the idea of fractions with other denominators, e.g. fifths, eighths. Examples then emerge where two fractions mean the same thing; thus a strip of paper divided into eight parts of which two are taken is the same as the strip divided into four and one part taken.

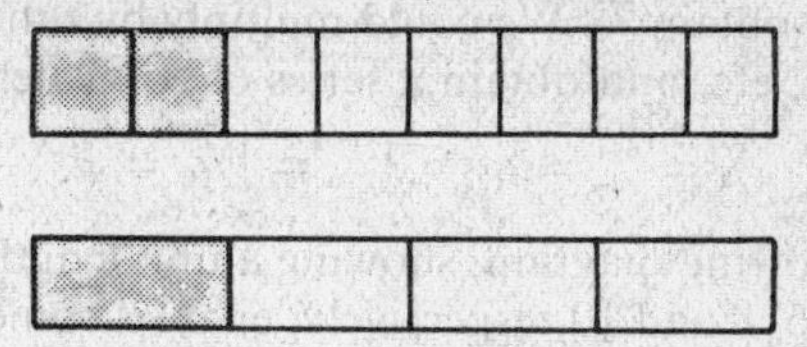

30. How one quarter equals two eighths.

It is seen that $\frac{2}{8}$ represents the same fraction as $\frac{1}{4}$. In Fig. 29, where a set of twelve counters is partitioned, it can be seen that $\frac{1}{4}$ is the same part of the whole as $\frac{3}{12}$. This is the idea of the *equivalence of fractions* and is probably the most important concept that primary children should achieve in their work on fractions.

If a line is taken and divided into halves, quarters and eighths (i.e. halving repeatedly), the equivalences emerge.

0 1

			$\frac{1}{2}$				$\frac{2}{2}$
	$\frac{1}{4}$		$\frac{2}{4}$		$\frac{3}{4}$		$\frac{4}{4}$
$\frac{1}{8}$	$\frac{2}{8}$	$\frac{3}{8}$	$\frac{4}{8}$	$\frac{5}{8}$	$\frac{6}{8}$	$\frac{7}{8}$	$\frac{8}{8}$

31 Halving repeatedly to show equivalences.

Clearly $\frac{1}{2} = \frac{2}{4} = \frac{4}{8}$ $\frac{1}{4} = \frac{2}{8}$ $\frac{3}{4} = \frac{6}{8}$
and $1 = \frac{2}{2} = \frac{4}{4} = \frac{8}{8}$

It will be seen that a fraction equivalent to another fraction is obtained by multiplying (or dividing) numerator and denominator of the original fraction by the same number. Thus, multiplying numerator and denominator of $\frac{3}{4}$ by 2 we obtain $\frac{6}{8}$. We could multiply by other numbers, e.g. 3, 4, 5, etc. and obtain a series of equivalent fractions:

$$\frac{3}{4} = \frac{6}{8} = \frac{9}{12} = \frac{12}{16} = \frac{15}{20} = \ldots$$

The following diagram, showing a unit length divided by 2, 3, 4, 5, 6, 8 and 10 respectively, enables some equivalent fractions to be picked out by inspection.

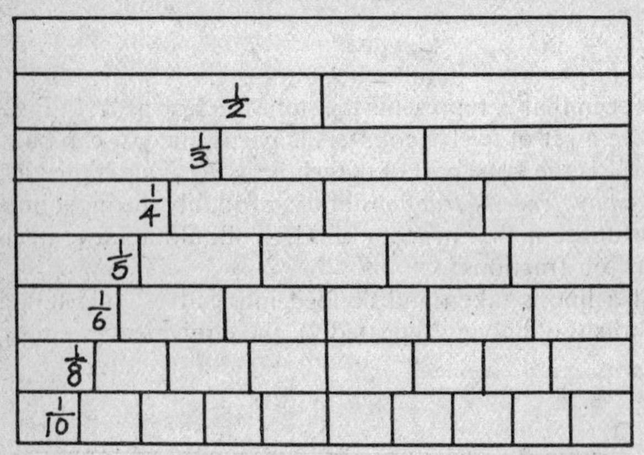

32. Dividing a length by various different numbers enables some equivalent fractions to be picked out visually.

FINDING FRACTIONAL PARTS

The work so far described is directed particularly to familiarizing the child with fractions, and parents can help their children's understanding by stressing the idea of fractions in normal everyday life. An apple is cut into two halves; the halves are cut again, forming quarters. The newspaper has 20 pages, so one page is $\frac{1}{20}$th of the whole. If there are 12 panes of glass in the window, one pane is a twelfth. Many examples present themselves.

The next stage of the work occurs when finding a fraction of a certain number or quantity. Money provides a good practical approach in this case: what is a half of tenpence? What is a quarter of £1? The idea of the inverse is evident here. Since twice 5p is 10p, 5p is half of 10p; £1 is four times 25p, so 25p is a quarter of £1. Measurement generally is valuable in this work, e.g. the programme starts on TV in a quarter of an hour; how many minutes will that be?; we wish to make a half quantity of a cookery recipe, what quantities of ingredients do we take?

A quarter of an hour is found by dividing sixty minutes by 4 to obtain 15 minutes. To find ¾ of an hour, we then multiply the 15 minutes by 3 to obtain 45 minutes. This brings out the idea that *¾ of 60 is 3 times* (¼ of 60), or in other words that $\frac{3}{4} = 3 \times \frac{1}{4}$. This idea is reinforced by work with sets or with number apparatus. An example of the use of counters is shown below.

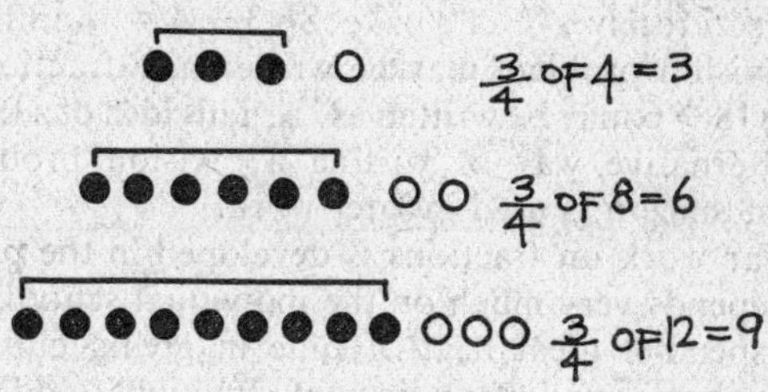

33. Using counters to find three quarters.

Children having understanding difficulties at this stage should do lots of work with counters along these lines. The number line may be used also.

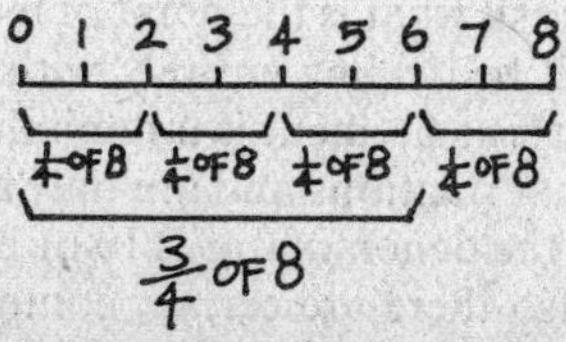

34. Using a number line to find three quarters.

FRACTIONS AS A SYMBOL OF DIVISION

We have already met examples such as: eight counters is 4 times as many as two counters, so two counters is $\frac{1}{4}$ of eight counters. Or in symbols: $\frac{1}{4}$ of $8 = 2$ and $8 \div 4 = 2$, the last equation being simply another way of writing $8 = 4 \times 2$.

It would seem, therefore, that $\frac{1}{4}$ is another way of writing 1 divided by 4. What of a fraction such as $\frac{3}{4}$? As an example, consider 3 cakes shared between 4 people, A, B, C and D.

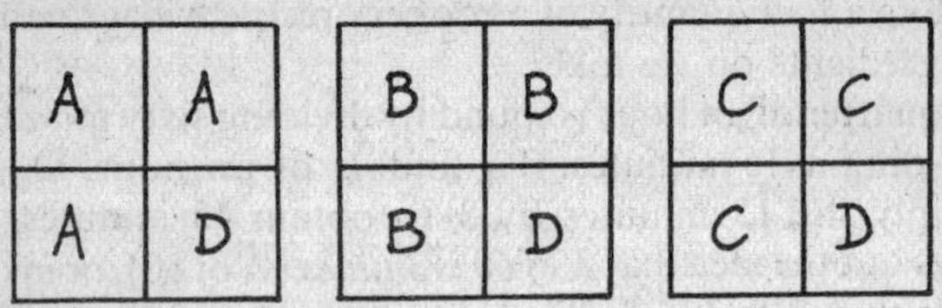

A	A
A	D

B	B
B	D

C	C
C	D

35. Three cakes divided among four people.

Each person receives $\frac{3}{4}$ of a cake. So $3 \div 4 = \frac{3}{4}$ and we see that a division problem may be written as a fraction. For example, $18 \div 6$ may be written as $\frac{18}{6}$. This idea of a fraction as an alternative way of writing a division problem is important since it is used in later work.

How far work on fractions is developed in the primary school depends very much on the individual school. Some schools spend a great deal of time in giving children a thorough basic understanding of fractions and spend correspondingly less time on calculations involving fractions, whereas other schools progress more quickly onto the calculation work. The whole matter of work on fractions has been reconsidered in recent years, particularly in the light of the decimalisation of money and our weights and measures. Some people may ask what is the point of teaching fractions when children will be dealing entirely with decimals?

The answer to this statement is a reminder that decimals are, in fact, decimal fractions and are only a particular type of fraction where the denominator is 10 or powers of 10, i.e. 100, 1000, etc. Also there are certain common fractions in everyday use which do not fit well into the decimal system.

For example, we often have to deal with thirds, but these cannot be expressed exactly in decimals, giving recurring decimals. Fractions, therefore, are still taught in schools, but not to the extent of the more complicated fractional calculations that were taught in the past which seemed to be devised more as a mathematical exercise than as something likely to be met in real life. The fractions that are used today are the more common ones, which do have practical applications.

There are times when the numerator of a fraction is larger than the denominator, e.g. $^{11}/_{4}$. A fraction such as this is called an *improper fraction*, and since it represents the division of 11 by 4, we may divide, to obtain 2 whole units and 3 quarters, i.e. $2^{3}/_{4}$. We call a number such as this, which has an integral part and a fractional part, a *mixed number*. In working with fractions it is sometimes necessary to change mixed numbers into improper fractions and vice versa. For example, $3^{1}/_{5}$ would be written $^{16}/_{5}$ and $4^{3}/_{8}$ is written as $^{35}/_{8}$.

THE FOUR RULES AND FRACTIONS

Remembering what has been said above, not all schools will cover the four rules as applied to fractions; some may deal with addition and subtraction of fractions but leave multiplication and division for later work in the secondary school.

The addition and subtraction of fractions makes use of equivalent fractions. When two fractions are being added or subtracted, it is essential that both have the same denominator so that we are adding or subtracting the same kind of fractional part, i.e. they are both quarters, or twelfths, or sixteenths, etc. As a simple example, suppose $^{1}/_{4}$ and $^{1}/_{3}$ are to be added. From the earlier work on equivalent fractions:

$$^{1}/_{4} = ^{2}/_{8} = ^{3}/_{12} = ^{4}/_{16} = ^{5}/_{20} = ^{6}/_{24} = \ldots$$
$$^{1}/_{3} = ^{2}/_{6} = ^{3}/_{9} = ^{4}/_{12} = ^{5}/_{15} = ^{6}/_{18} = ^{7}/_{21} = ^{8}/_{24} = \ldots$$

Comparing the two lines, we could change both fractions to twelfths or to twenty-fourths, and obviously there are other possibilities with denominators greater than 24, e.g. 36, 48. There is no point in having larger numbers than is really necessary, so we use twelfths and write:

$$\frac{1}{4} + \frac{1}{3} = \frac{3}{12} + \frac{4}{12} = \frac{7}{12}$$

The first step in this work, therefore, is to find the denominator into which the two given denominators will divide exactly; we call this new denominator (12 in the case above) the *common denominator* of the two fractions.

As a further example, consider

$$\frac{4}{5} - \frac{3}{8}$$

The common denominator in this case is 40, which is the smallest number into which both 5 and 8 will divide. Hence $\frac{4}{5} - \frac{3}{8} = \frac{32}{40} - \frac{15}{40} = \frac{17}{40}$

In these two examples, the common denominator in each case has been the product of the two original denominators. This will always provide a common denominator, but it may not be the smallest number which could be the common denominator. For example, in the following, the product would be 48, whereas 24 is suitable:

$$\frac{5}{6} + \frac{3}{8} = \frac{20}{24} + \frac{9}{24} = \frac{29}{24}$$

The answer is an improper fraction in this case, and it could be changed to a mixed number, $1\frac{5}{24}$. In the recording of this work, some schools choose to have the pupils set down their work with the common denominator set under a line, over which are written the appropriate numerators, as follows:

$$\frac{5}{6} + \frac{3}{8} = \frac{20 + 9}{24} = \frac{29}{24}$$

This method may not be so easily understood by the pupil, since the equivalences of the fractions $\frac{5}{6}$ and $\frac{20}{24}$ and of $\frac{3}{8}$ and $\frac{9}{24}$ are not brought out so clearly. In fact, a child using this latter method may learn it as a rule without really understanding what is taking place. If a child using that method is having difficulty with understanding, there may be a case for having him use the other method, first revising equivalent fractions.

At the primary level, the fractions used in examples will be fairly simple with denominators which are easy to handle, so that there should be little difficulty in finding the common denominator. In the case of more complicated fractions, there are methods of finding the appropriate denominator by obtaining the *lowest common multiple* of the numbers which constitute the denominators. The lowest common multiple of a set of numbers is the smallest number into which each member of the set will divide exactly. In the example above, 24 is the lowest common multiple of 6 and 8, so that we have been finding lowest common multiples, mainly by inspection.

Where mixed numbers are involved in addition and subtration calculations, the method is to split the numbers into their integral and fractional parts and operate accordingly, as in these two examples:

(a) $3\frac{2}{5}+4\frac{1}{3}=3+4+\frac{2}{5}+\frac{1}{3}$
$=7+\frac{6}{15}+\frac{5}{15}$
$=7\frac{11}{15}$

(b) $6\frac{1}{8}-2\frac{3}{4}=6-2+\frac{1}{8}-\frac{3}{4}$
$=4+\frac{1}{8}-\frac{6}{8}$
$=3+\frac{9}{8}-\frac{6}{8}$ (see below)
$=3\frac{3}{8}$

In the third line of example (b), the 4 units of the previous line have been reduced to 3 and the extra unit (or $\frac{8}{8}$) has been added to the $\frac{1}{8}$ to make $\frac{9}{8}$ so that $\frac{6}{8}$ could be subtracted from it.

Mention may be made of multiplication of fractions, although many schools will not proceed far with this work. It requires understanding of difficult concepts, which may be beyond many children at this stage. The only way to give real meaning to fraction multiplication is through the use of the word 'of' as synonymous with '×', as in the case of 'What is $\frac{1}{2}$ of 4?' The answer could be found from partitioning; $\frac{1}{2}$ means partitioning the set into two equal parts. A child may have a square sheet of paper and cut it into two equal parts; then taking one of the halves, cut this into two equal parts again. So, by taking $\frac{1}{2}$ of $\frac{1}{2}$, the result is $\frac{1}{4}$. The result may be repeated, for example taking $\frac{1}{3}$ of $\frac{1}{2}$ to obtain $\frac{1}{6}$, and we see that the results in such cases are obtained by multiplying the denominators. Replacing 'of' by the multiplication sign gives results such as:

$$\tfrac{1}{3} \times \tfrac{1}{4} = \tfrac{1}{12} \qquad \tfrac{1}{5} \times \tfrac{1}{2} = \tfrac{1}{10}$$

These examples could be demonstrated by using a diagram similar to Fig. 31. Another approach employs the idea of multiplication as repeated addition, as follows:

(a) $\tfrac{1}{4} + \tfrac{1}{4} + \tfrac{1}{4} = \tfrac{3}{4}$
or $3 \times \tfrac{1}{4} = \tfrac{3}{4}$

(b) $\tfrac{2}{3} + \tfrac{2}{3} + \tfrac{2}{3} + \tfrac{2}{3} = \tfrac{8}{3}$
or $4 \times \tfrac{2}{3} = \tfrac{8}{3}$

Cases such as these illustrate the method of multiplying the numerator of the fraction by the whole number.

The division of a fraction by a whole number may be explained with the example above, where half a sheet of paper was halved again; this could be regarded as the half-sheet divided by 2, i.e. $\tfrac{1}{2} \div 2 = \tfrac{1}{4}$. Or, for the example given above where $\tfrac{1}{3}$ of $\tfrac{1}{2} = \tfrac{1}{6}$, we could have $\tfrac{1}{2} \div 3 = \tfrac{1}{6}$.

Examples requiring the division of one fraction by another are best explained by the use of the inverse; this is dealt with in Chapter 11 (Section E, page 171).

DECIMAL FRACTIONS

The increased use of decimals in our everyday life, especially with regard to weights and measures, has led schools to spend less time than formerly on vulgar fractions and to devote more time to decimal fractions, or decimals as they are usually called. The name 'decimal fraction' is used here to emphasize that decimals are a particular type of fraction where the denominator has to be 10 or a power of 10, i.e. 100, 1000, 10000, etc. Also, of course, we have a special way of writing these fractions; instead of $\tfrac{3}{10}$, we write 0·3 and for $\tfrac{23}{100}$ we write 0·23. This approach is similar to that for vulgar fractions, since to represent 0·3, we would partition the set into 10 equal parts and take 3 of them.

The more usual approach to decimals, however, is by extending the placing of figures in our number system. If we have a number such as 235, we know that the 5 represents 5 units, the 3 represents 3 tens and the 2 represents 2 hundreds. As explained earlier, children sometimes put these figures into columns, headed 'units', 'tens', and 'hundreds', thus:

hundreds	*tens*	*units*
2	3	5
6	6	6

A second number, 666, has been written in the columns; notice that, as we move to the right, the value of each 6 is divided by ten, i.e. their value is 600, 60 and 6. Suppose, therefore, that we move into an extra column to the right, then this column would represent tenths of a whole unit, and if we moved a further column to the right, it would represent hundredths of a unit and so on.

hundreds	*tens*	*units*	*tenths*	*hundredths*	*thousandths*
6	6	6	6	6	6

Since we seldom use columns in normal working, we have to indicate the separation between units and tenths and we do this by inserting a decimal point, thus:

666·666

The decimal point is a reference point showing where the units column lies. Thus with 235· 64, we immediately read this as 'Two hundred and thirty five point six four'. (Notice that we say 'six four' and not 'sixty four' because the six does not represent sixty).

Having established our system of decimals, we proceed to operate on it in a similar manner to whole numbers. For addition we must keep units under units, tens under tens, tenths under tenths and so on:

$$\begin{array}{r} 235{\cdot}64 \\ 18{\cdot}7 \\ 165{\cdot}39 \\ 208{\cdot}06 \\ \underline{88{\cdot}40} \\ 716{\cdot}19 \end{array}$$

And the same is true for subtraction. The decimal points must always be in line.

If multiplication and division involving decimals is taught in the primary school, it will be of a simple nature in all probability. Thus multiplication will be that of a decimal by a whole number. This is performed exactly as multiplication of whole numbers, except the decimal point must be inserted to indicate the units place. An example is 32·63 × 8:

$$\begin{array}{r} 32{\cdot}63 \\ \times \quad\ \ 8 \\ \hline 261{\cdot}04 \end{array}$$

The same is true of division by a whole number: follow the general rules and take care to insert the decimal point, e.g. 25·56 ÷ 6.

$$\begin{array}{r} 4{\cdot}26 \\ 6\ \overline{)\ 25{\cdot}56} \\ \underline{24} \\ 1\,5 \\ \underline{1\,2} \\ 36 \\ \underline{36} \end{array}$$

In the case of division, we may add as many noughts as we wish to the end of the decimal part, e.g. 61·8 ÷ 8:

$$\begin{array}{r} 7{\cdot}725 \\ 8\ \overline{)\ 61{\cdot}800} \\ \underline{56} \\ 5\,8 \\ \underline{5\,6} \\ 20 \\ \underline{16} \\ 40 \\ \underline{40} \end{array}$$

Decimal currency and the increasing use of decimal measures means that there are plenty of practical situations which can form a basis of work on decimals, and children having difficulty with any of this work could use coins to perform the calculations. The coins are best restricted to 1 penny, and 10 pence, and the notes to £1 and £10 (paper representations, of course!). In fact, children are so familiar with our system of coinage that this is sometimes used as a means of introducing the idea of decimals.

There are certain parts of the work which can cause difficulty. Firstly, children should always be encouraged to put a 0 before the decimal point when there is no further figure there, e.g. 0·57 rather than ·57. We do this, of course, when expressing 57 pence as pounds, i.e. £0·57. This practice can help to avoid mistakes. Secondly, children often have difficulty over the relative value of decimals, e.g. is 0·9 less than 0·15? Errors arise from a lack of understanding of place value as applied to the decimal positions. 15 is greater than 9 (they reason), so 0·15 must be greater than 0·9, forgetting that the 9 represents $^9/_{10}$ths of a whole and that the 15 is not 'fifteen' but $^1/_{10}$th together with $^5/_{100}$ths. The way to illustrate this is to arrange the numbers under column headings (as in the case of 666·666 on page 87) when the actual value of the 9, 1 and 5 can be read off, or the two numbers may be represented on a diagram like this:

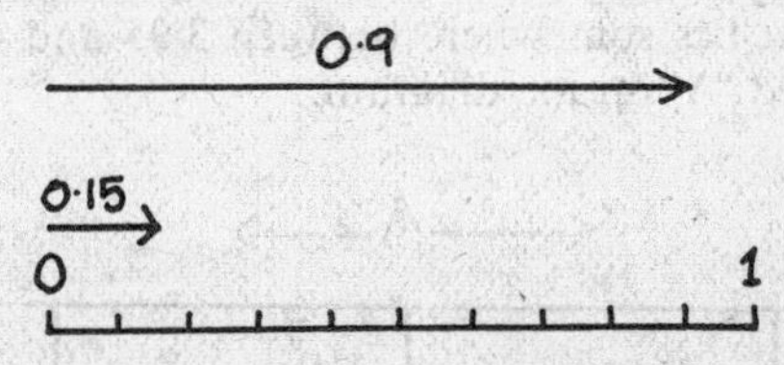

36. Diagram to show that 0.9 is greater than 0.15.

One source of error is the fact that we tend to drop the noughts at the end of a decimal number in most cases. Not so with money, where we write £0·90 and £0·15, which people read as 90 pence and 15 pence and confusion does not arise.

The only time that we write decimals in the form 0·90 is when we wish to indicate that there is accuracy to the second decimal place.

DEGREE OF ACCURACY

This is a useful point to consider the accuracy with which we express quantities in number, since it forms a link with the chapter which follows on measurement. A man will cut a piece of wood which he will say is exactly 2 metres long; a child will draw a line with a ruler and say it is exactly 4 cm long. But are they 'exactly' what they are supposed to be? They represent the degree of accuracy with the tools available, and to some extent with the person's ability to use them. But if we have a more accurate means of measurement, might we not find that the wood measures 1·99 metres, or the line measures 4·01 cm?

Suppose a child used a ruler marked in millimetres and worked very carefully. Then 1 millimetre short of 4 cm would be 3·9 cm and 1 millimetre too much would be 4·1 cm. The child would take great care to measure as close to 4·0 as possible and if, say, the line ended at a point closer to 3·9 than 4, he would call it 3·9 cm long. Where does 'closer' begin? Obviously it will be at a point which is less than half way between the two, i.e. nearer 3·9 than 3·95. Similarly for the other side of 4. So the best we can say is that his 'exact' measurement lies somewhere between 3·95 and 4·05 – the space marked 'A' on the diagram.

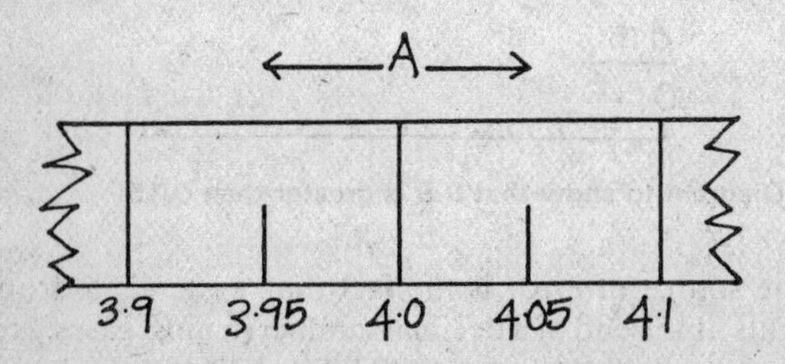

37. Accuracy of measurement.

It is the argument embodied here which lies behind the methods of expressing decimal quantities to a given number of places. Suppose a number 6·48 has to be expressed to the nearest one decimal place; is it nearer to 6·4 or 6·5? Since it is more than 6·45, it is nearer the latter and to one decimal place it is 6·5. On the other hand, 6·42, to one decimal place, will be 6·4. In the case of 6·45, the usual convention is to regard this as 6·5, to one decimal place. We call this process *rounding* to a given number of decimal places, and speak of 'rounding up' and 'rounding down'. So 3·27 is rounded up to 3·3 and 4·12 is rounded down to 4·1, when writing them to one decimal place. Rounding of whole numbers was explained in the previous chapter.

The significance of writing 0·90 should now be clear. To write 0·9 indicates accuracy to one decimal place, whereas 0·90 indicates accuracy to 2 decimal places. Thus we would say that 0·897 is 0·90 to 2 decimal places. A child having difficulty with work such as this should be encouraged to work out the problem on a number line or a graduated ruler.

MULTIPLICATION AND DIVISION BY 10

If we multiply 40 by 10 we obtain 400; if we multiply 0·04 by 10 we obtain 0·4; if we divide 0·04 by 10, the answer is 0·004. We can set out similar results in a table:

Multiply by 10	*Original number*	*Divide by 10*
0·4	0·04	0·004
0·025	0·0025	0·00025
2·63	0·263	0·0263
158·6	15·86	1·586

The results show clearly that when we multiply by 10, the figures move one place to the left with respect to the decimal point; if we divide by 10, the figures move one place to the right with respect to the decimal point. Notice that it is wrong to say, as some people do, that the decimal point moves; the decimal point is always fixed, since it indicates where the units column lies. This is well illustrated by expressing a given number of millimetres in centimetres, decimetres, metres, dekametres, hectometres and kilometres, since each of these units of measurement is ten times the previous one. So we have, for example:

$$\begin{aligned} & 123456 \text{ mm} \\ = & \ 12345{\cdot}6 \text{ cm} \\ = & \ 1234{\cdot}56 \text{ dm} \\ = & \ 123{\cdot}456 \text{ m} \\ = & \ 12{\cdot}3456 \text{ Dm} \\ = & \ 1{\cdot}23456 \text{ Hm} \\ = & \ 0{\cdot}123456 \text{ Km} \end{aligned}$$

What has been said for multiplication and division by 10 applies in an extended manner to multiplication and division by 100 (i.e. 10×10), 1000 (i.e. $10 \times 10 \times 10$) and so on, the figures being moved the appropriate number of places in each case.

PERCENTAGES

Another way in which fractional parts may be expressed is as a percentage. As the name (per cent, i.e. per 100) implies, all percentages are one-hundredth parts of a whole. Thus when we speak of 7 per cent (or 7%) we mean $\frac{7}{100}$ of the whole. Percentages can often be reduced to simpler fractions. Thus 25 per cent is $\frac{25}{100}$, which can be reduced to the equivalent fraction $\frac{1}{4}$. So $25\% = \frac{1}{4}$. As a further example:

$$32\% = \frac{32}{100} = \frac{8}{25}$$

Notice that 100 per cent is equivalent to 1. Hence if we say that a class at school has 100 per cent attendance on a particular day, we mean that all the children were present. Also percentages over 100 per cent, when changed to fractions, will have an integral and a fractional part, i.e. will be a mixed number. For example, 125 per cent will equal $1\frac{1}{4}$ and 317 per cent will equal $3\frac{17}{100}$.

If we wish to express a fraction as a percentage, we require the equivalent number of parts of a hundred, or, in other words, to find the equivalent fraction with denominator 100. To find $\frac{2}{5}$ as a percentage, find $\frac{2}{5}$ of 100, i.e. $\frac{2}{5} \times 100$; the answer is 40% (or by equivalent fractions, $\frac{2}{5} = \frac{40}{100}$). Similarly $\frac{3}{8}$ as a percentage is $\frac{3}{8} \times 100$, i.e. $37\frac{1}{2}\%$.

The approach outlined above puts emphasis on the fractional aspect of a percentage and it is important that children should understand this in their early work on this topic. If they do, later work will be much simplified and better understood. Otherwise percentages come to be regarded as something entirely different, requiring a fresh series of techniques. Even at secondary level, many children have difficulty with work on percentages, the cause being the failure to understand that it is merely another way of expressing a fraction. A child having difficulties with this work may be having problems with this basic understanding. An extension of Fig. 31 (page 79) for equivalent fractions may be helpful, where an additional line divided into 100 parts is added; from the figure, fractions and their equivalent percentages may be read off.

If the work above has been understood, there should be little difficulty in dealing with practical problems where a percentage is required. As an example, suppose that 4 children are absent from a class of 32, what percentage is this? Since percentages are a form of fraction, we find what fraction of children is absent; this is $\frac{4}{32}$. We then express this fraction as an equivalent percentage, i.e.

$$\frac{4}{32} \times 100 = 12\frac{1}{2} \text{ per cent.}$$

It is better if children are encouraged to develop and use the idea of percentages in this way, rather than be given rules such as 'put the decrease (or increase) over the original quantity and multiply by 100'.

As with fractions and decimals, at the primary level the most important thing is that children should become familiar with the idea of percentages rather than have to work complicated calculations, and the equivalence of certain simple percentages with their fractions should be known. For example, 25 per cent, 50 per cent and 75 per cent should be recognized immediately as $\frac{1}{4}$, $\frac{1}{2}$ and $\frac{3}{4}$. The value of 10 per cent as $\frac{1}{10}$ should be known because it gives a whole series of equivalences by simple multiplication, e.g. 20% = $\frac{2}{10}$, 30% = $\frac{3}{10}$, etc. There are plenty of opportunities for parents to make children aware of percentages while out shopping. Shops frequently have offers of 'Ten per cent off', '25% reductions', '10% deposit' and so on. Questions such as 'What fraction is that?' immediately present themselves and in the case of fairly simple prices, it should be possible for the child to work out mentally how much is being saved by a particular offer, or what the new price will be.

EQUIVALENCE OF FRACTIONS, DECIMALS AND PERCENTAGES

Since fractions, decimals and percentages are different ways of expressing the same idea of a part of something, the links between the three should be thoroughly understood and the child should be able to translate one into the other.

Changing *fractions into decimals* follows immediately from the fact – mentioned earlier – that a fraction may be regarded as a way of expressing a division operation. Thus $\frac{3}{4}$ is a way of writing '3 divided by 4' and doing this division:

$$\begin{array}{r} 0{\cdot}75 \\ 4\;\overline{)\;3{\cdot}00} \\ \underline{2\,8} \\ 20 \\ \underline{20} \end{array}$$

Hence $\frac{3}{4}$ = 0·75.

Certain fractions will not work out exactly and their answers are usually given to a certain number of decimal places, e.g. $\frac{2}{7}$ = 0·28571 . . . or 0·29 to two decimal places.

Changing *decimals into fractions* is achieved by writing the decimal as a fraction and reducing it to the simplest equivalent fraction. Thus 0·45 = $^{45}/_{100}$ = $^{9}/_{20}$.

Changing *fractions to percentages* and vice versa has been explained above.

Changing *decimals to percentages* and vice versa is straightforward, since the first two places of decimals represent hundredths and percentages are also hundredths. So, for example, 0·37 is equivalent to 37 per cent, and 0·82 is equivalent to 82 per cent. For the reverse process, 54 per cent is 0·54 and 7 per cent is 0·07. For more complicated examples, the rule still applies; thus 0·3475 is equal to 34·75 per cent and 26½ per cent is the same as 0·265.

SUGGESTIONS FOR HELP

Suggestions have been made at various points in the chapter and the work has been explained in detail since it is important for the child to have an understanding of the principles underlying the work. Much more work on fractions and decimals is done in the secondary school and this work is built on the basic work done here.

Children experiencing difficulty need to spend much time on initial work of representing fractions by shading figures, cutting paper, working with counters or drawing and partitioning sets; this work is outlined in the early part of the chapter. In fact, much of the difficulty with fractions can be resolved by the use of appropriate diagrams similar to those appearing in this chapter. Finally, remember that the work covered in this chapter is spread over the whole of the primary school years and some would most likely not be covered until the secondary school. It is important, therefore, to pick out the appropriate parts of the work as far as your child is concerned.

7
MEASUREMENT

METRIC AND IMPERIAL MEASURE

This preliminary note is necessary because of the confusion in this country over the use of metric measures (i.e. metres, litres, kilogrammes, etc.) and the old Imperial measures (i.e. yards, pints, pounds, etc.).

Some years ago a date was fixed by which the country should turn over entirely to metric measures. That date has long passed and, for various reasons, the change to metrication is still incomplete. However, at the time when the statement was made, most schools and examination boards, anticipating the alteration, changed to metric measures only. Consequently, measurement in schools is now based on the metric system. The fact that children find Imperial measures still in use outside the school, can only be a source of confusion as long as it lasts. This creates a problem for schools which is resolved in different ways.

However, in schools all measurement will be in metric measure, as will all calculation. Obviously, as children are introduced to the various units, they will handle them so that they know, for example, the length which corresponds to a metre. But as long as Imperial measures are used, children should also have an appreciation of the size of these measures too, although restricted to those still in common use. Some ideas of corresponding metric and Imperial measures would be given, but not problems on converting from one system to another. Thus, from experience, children would learn that a kilogramme is just over 2 lb, or a metre just over a yard. Ultimately, mention of Imperial units will end as the country turns completely to metric measure.

MEASUREMENT AND NUMBER WORK

It was pointed out in the chapter on early work in mathematics, that the child's first introduction to measure was by the use of non-standard units. A desk-top is measured as a certain number of hand spans, a room is so many strides long and a milk bottle holds a particular number of egg-cupfuls of water. It can be seen, even at this stage, that measurement provides a starting point for number work.

As standard units are introduced, measurement provides further examples of calculation of varying complexity. It has been emphasized already that the key to understanding mathematics comes through dealing with practical situations, where the pupil can see and handle materials which form a basis for his calculation work. Measurement is probably the most valuable source of such practical work.

In the home there are many examples of measurement in which children can be involved. Weights and measures are used in the kitchen, clocks measure time, electricity and gas meters register quantities used, the speedometer of a car registers its speed and the mileometer the distance travelled. Buying new curtains and carpets is a source of measurement and calculation. Money may be considered under the heading of measurement (it is a measure of spending power) and can also lead to calculation. The more young children can be given such practical experiences from their everyday surroundings, the better it will be for their mathematical development. Teachers in the classroom make use of the environment and this work can be continued outside school. Ask the child what has been done at school today, then see if reference cannot be made to some similar situation about the home.

The number line has been shown to be of value when children are dealing with number work and many scales of measurement in everyday use are applications of the number line. An ordinary ruler or a tape measure are obvious examples, but anything with a scale – such as a thermometer – incorporates the idea of the number line. The point to remember is that when we wish to work on a number line, it could equally well be one of these scales, thereby bringing variety and interest to the work.

Measurement should not be considered as a separate topic for study, but should be integrated with the number work. This is particularly true as work on measurement develops in the metric system where all weights and measures are to base 10, like the number system. It is no longer necessary in school work for the child to remember *twelve* inches in a foot, *three* feet in a yard, *eight* pints in a quart, *sixteen* ounces in a pound, and so on. With the metric system there is one multiple only – *ten*.

First measurements using standard units (as opposed to pacing or spanning a length, etc.) will deal with whole units and can take place alongside number work with whole numbers. A child can accept measurements such as 214 cm and add, subtract, multiply and divide them without difficulty if he can do the corresponding number work. When the idea of decimals is introduced, conversion to other units can be made quickly; 214 cm becomes 2·14 metres and calculation involving decimals is quickly applied to metric measure.

If a child is having difficulty with number work and needs some practice, instead of providing endless 'sums' to be worked in a book, look for sources of calculation in measurement, thereby making the work interesting and realistic. Get a child to measure the rise and tread of one step of a staircase, then find the length of carpet needed to cover the whole of the stairs. Find the perimeter of a room. Measure a paving stone in the garden path and then find the total length of the path. Measure the overall length of a sliced loaf and work out the thickness of a slice; some children may be intrigued to use the same technique to find the thickness of the page of a book. Count the number of sweets in a pack of given weight and then calculate the weight of one sweet. These are examples of everyday sources of calculation practice which also help with a child's understanding of the application of mathematics.

ESTIMATION

It is essential, of course, that a child should see and handle the measures with which he is dealing. There is the danger that many calculations involving measure may be performed correctly without knowing what the measures are. When a child talks about a gramme, does he realize what a small weight this is? Does he appreciate how much is a litre or what length is approximately a metre? Experience in handling such quantities is as important as being able to perform calculations involving them.

From this develops the ability to estimate lengths, weights or other measures. Roughly how high is the room? What is the approximate weight of this box? How many litres will this jug hold? These are the sort of questions which will help a child in this work. A valuable approach is to know the measurement of certain things and be able to apply this standard to the problem. For example, if a child knows his own height in metres and wishes to estimate the height of a room, he only needs to imagine how many times that particular height would be equivalent to the room height. Other useful measures to know include the length of the child's stride and the span of his hand. The weight or capacity of some everyday object in the house could similarly form a useful basis for estimation. Practice in estimating could take the form of a game, first guessing what a thing measures, then actually measuring it.

The value of this work as part of general education will be appreciated; it is something that will stand the child in good stead as he grows older. The most important way of checking calculations is to ask if the answer is reasonable and when measurement is involved the ability to be able to say if the answer obtained seems reasonable can save many errors. A child must realize that his mathematics is dealing with real things and not just figures on a piece of paper.

Some points are given next which relate to particular

types of measurement. These are mainly for guidance and reference where children are having difficulty with a particular problem.

TIME

Time is a measure which is not metric, of course, but it need not enter into a child's work on calculation to any great extent. Calculation with respect to time is mainly addition and subtraction when it does occur, e.g. 'It is now 10.15 and I will meet you in 40 minutes.'; 'How many days to Easter?'

The main help that a parent can give is in developing the ability to read time from clocks and dates from the calendar. There are plenty of practical applications which can be found such as: 'We will go out at 2 o'clock; how many minutes time is that?' or 'How many days is it to your birthday?' One difficulty with clock time is the way we speak of the number of minutes past or to the hour and our use of quarters and halves, e.g. quarter past two. Digital clocks and watches have also brought complications. But all this is as much a part of general education and language development as it is mathematics and so should receive attention.

MASS OR WEIGHT

Some mathematics courses now speak of mass rather than weight and strictly speaking this is the correct term, although in everyday use we tend to speak of weight. The mass is the amount of material in a body, whereas the weight is the attraction of the earth on that mass. In everyday life about the home and in shops, the two are virtually interchangeable, but with the present technological advances new situations arise when there is a difference between the two. The mass of a lunar module, for example, is the same on the earth as it is on the moon, but the weight is different because the attraction of the earth on objects at its surface is greater than the moon's attraction upon objects on its surface. Consequently it requires a much less powerful thrust to get the module off the moon's surface than it does off the earth's surface. Even at different parts of the earth's surface the weight of a given mass of material can vary, depending on how far it is from the earth's centre.

This variation in weight, of course, would only be measurable by some form of spring balance. The type of scales which balance the material against weights would show no change, since the weight of these weights would also vary from place to place.

Parents can help children doing this work by letting them weigh materials at home. If both balance scales (where weights are put on one pan to balance the material on the other) and dial scales (usually dependent on a spring mechanism) are available, so much the better. Children could help in the kitchen with weighing out materials; even if metric weights are not being used in the house, the experience is still of value.

AREA AND VOLUME

These are two difficult topics and calculation of areas and volumes in standard units is left until fairly late in the primary school course. However, from very early stages in the infant school, the basic concepts have to be understood Area is concerned with measuring a surface; volume with measuring a three-dimensional space.

In the earliest activity, the ideas arise from fitting shapes together. Cardboard or plastic shapes (squares or triangles, for example) are fitted together to make up a large shape and the number of pieces making up the shape are counted. The child may say that the shape is covered by eight triangles. Similar work can be done by fitting cubes together to form a solid. You will remember that in the case of measurement of length, first experiences were with non-standard units (e.g. spans, strides) and the same is true with area and volume.

With standard units of area, the definition is based on the amount of surface in a square of a given size. Thus a square centimetre is the space in a square whose sides measure one centimetre. Notice, however, that this is for the purpose of definition only and a square centimetre of area could be any shape provided the surface of that shape was the same as that of a square of side one centimetre. These ideas are developed from measuring shapes by counting squares which may be either drawn over the shape or on plastic sheet which is placed over the shape. The diagram shows this idea in use.

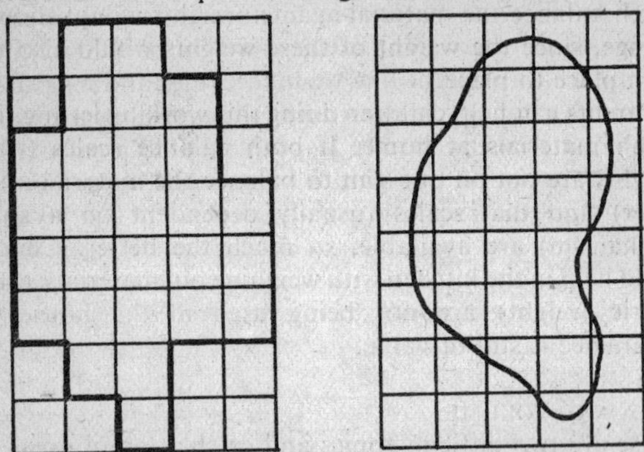

38. **Measuring area. The shape may or may not coincide with the squares.**

The area of a rectangle or square is a much easier problem and allows the use of an easy way of counting the square units; if there are four rows of squares with eight squares in a row, multiply 4 by 8 to find the area is 32 square centimetres; nowadays this is often written as 32 cm^2.

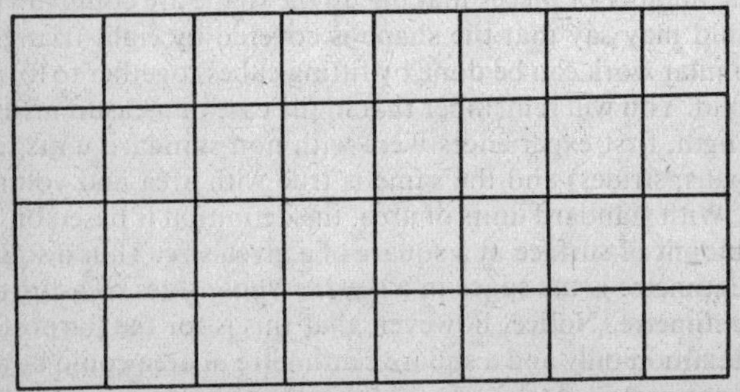

39. **A rectangle 4cm by 8cm.**

In this case the length and breadth have been measured in centimetres, then multiplied together. So we have the oft-quoted formula that 'area = length times breadth'. However, this is only true for a rectangle. For other shapes different formulae are developed. It should now be apparent that finding area requires some calculation. When finding the length of a straight line we take a ruler and measure it, but we have not got an instrument which will measure area. Instead we measure certain *lengths*, then do a calculation; this is why area and volume tend to be difficult topics for children.

In the case of volume, the general approach is the same as with area. Centimetre cubes are fitted together and counted. It is seen that the volume of a rectangular block (or cuboid as it is called) is obtained by multiplying together the length, breadth and height of the cuboid. What we are really doing is using a quick way to count the centimetre cubes. We then say that the volume is a certain number of cubic centimetres; in the case of the diagram below, it is 12 cubic centimetres (written 12 cm^3).

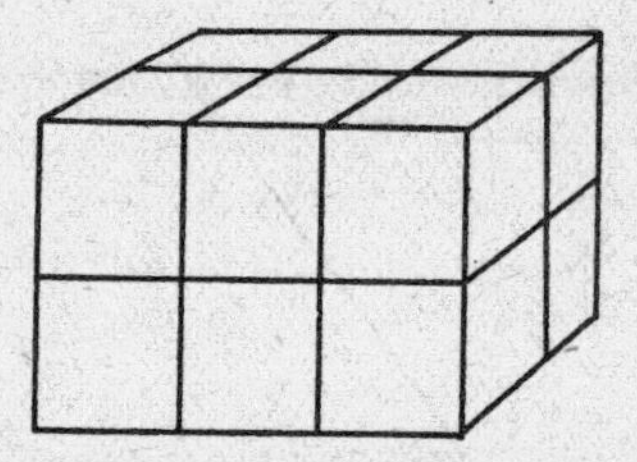

40. The volume of this is 12 cubic centimetres (cm^3).

ANGLE MEASUREMENT

The idea of an angle is another example where children often fail to grasp the basic concept and describe a particular development instead. For example, many children will describe an angle, wrongly, as two lines meeting at a point. The true definition is that it is a measure of turning.

When we cross a room we can measure the distance walked by using a tape measure; we are measuring length. If we turn to move in a different direction, then we need some measure of how far we have turned. Have we turned to face the way we came? or only partly turned so that we face another direction? It is this turning which makes the angle.

The first angles which children meet are a complete turn or revolution, a half-turn or straight angle, and a quarter-turn or right angle. The basic compass directions, North, East, South, West, give ideas of such turns. But the need for intermediate measurement leads to the idea of measuring angles in degrees, where a revolution is 360°, a straight angle is 180° and a right angle is 90°; other angles can also be measured.

Some terms which children meet are *acute* angles (angles less than 90°), *obtuse* angles (lying between 90° and 180°) and *reflex* angles (between 180° and 360°). When angles are drawn on paper, we see the 'two lines meeting at a point', but it is the turning between these lines, and not the lines, which makes the angle, so it is usual to insert a curved arrow to show the turn, e.g.

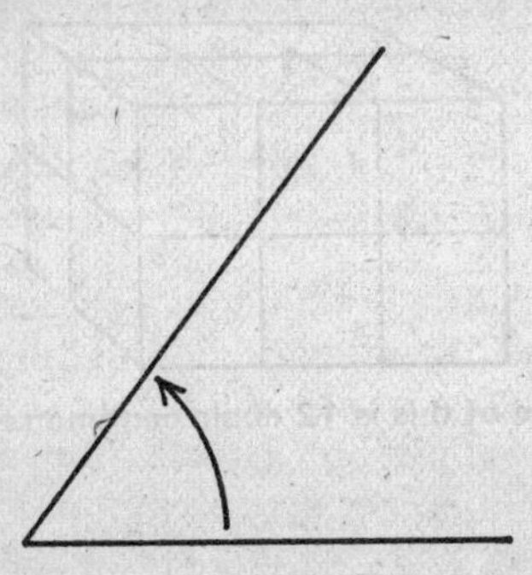

41. An angle with a curved arrow showing the turn.

Children need plenty of practice in the use of a protractor for measuring and constructing angles. Since the use of instruments needs almost personal tuition, a child may fail to achieve this skill, leading to later difficulties; this is a case where help from a parent can be extremely useful. The best type of protractor for a child is a completely circular one, and since degrees are very small units on a protractor, younger children may benefit from using a protractor which is only marked in ten degree or five degree intervals.

One difficulty with protractors is that scales read round from 0° in both clockwise and anticlockwise directions, this being necessary, of course, to cope with turning in either direction. When constructing or measuring an angle, the zero line (0°) should lie on a straight line with the centre of the protractor at one end of it. The degrees are then counted round according to which direction the turning is being measured. The diagram illustrates:

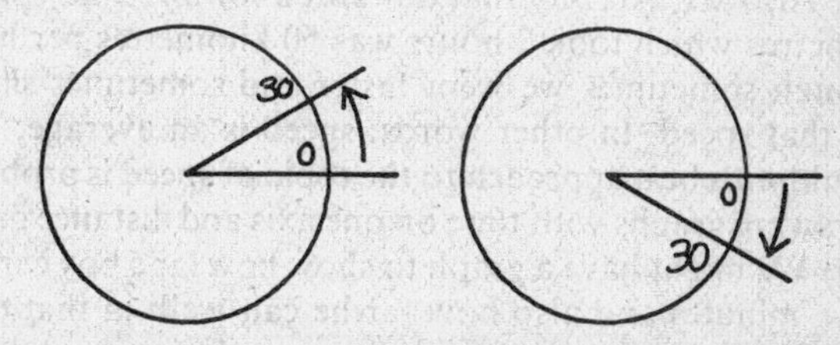

42. The angle is 30° and it may turn either way.

AVERAGES

This topic is considered at this point because of the next measurement – speed. Averages are more usually related to work in statistics where an average is called the *arithmetic mean*, or sometimes simply the mean. The idea of an average can arise from re-distributing things to give fair shares. For example, if three children have 5 sweets, 6 sweets and 10 sweets each, they have a total of 21 sweets and a fair share-out would give each child $^{21}/_{3}$, i.e. 7 sweets each. The idea of a 'middle value' may also arise from examples such as marks in a test or heights of a group of children. The calculation of an average is fairly simple and straightforward, but certain points should be appreciated by the child. Thus in the example of the sweets, initially no child has the average number of sweets; also some children have less than the average and some have more than the average. We cannot have the situation desired by the politician who said that everyone should have at least the average wage for the country!

The idea of an average is dealt with also in the chapter on graphical work.

SPEED

Speed is a fairly sophisticated topic since it involves two measures – distance and time. When driving a car, we may say that we are travelling at 60 kilometres per hour although we may only travel at that speed for a few seconds and not an hour. Also we may say that our speed for a journey of 100 kilometres which took 2 hours was 50 kilometres per hour, although sometimes we went faster and sometimes slower than that speed. In other words, speed is an average.

Children's best approach to the topic of speed is probably by drawing graphs with time on one axis and distance on the other. We might have a graph to show how far a boy can run in five minutes and also how far he can walk in that time. On such graphs, time is always shown on the horizontal axis. From the graph it can be seen that the higher the speed, the steeper is the graph.

Any calculations which children do on speed at the primary level should be fairly straightforward and will involve the relationship

$$\frac{\text{distance}}{\text{time}} = \text{speed.}$$

SUGGESTIONS FOR HELP

Suggestions have already been made of ways in which parents could help children with individual topics of measurement. It was stressed how valuable measurement can be in providing realistic examples involving calculation.

Parents could help children considerably by showing them how to use measuring instruments correctly. Many errors in

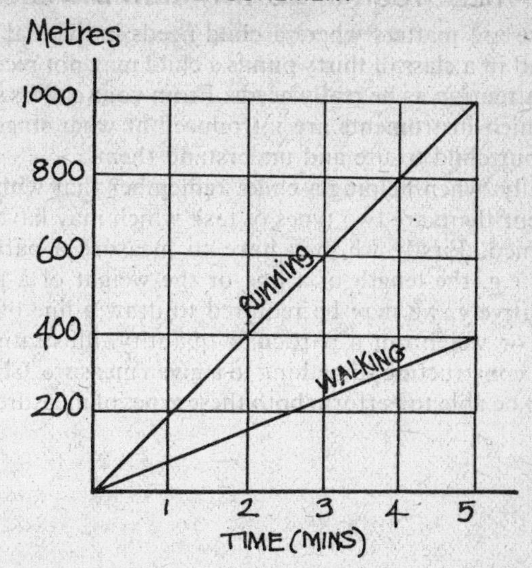

43. The graph shows that running is faster than walking.

measurement arise from incorrect use, particularly by wrong positioning of the instrument in the zero (i.e. 0) position, e.g. rulers, protractors.

The ability to read scales correctly is important, particularly involving small units which are not numbered, e.g. 27 on the scale below.

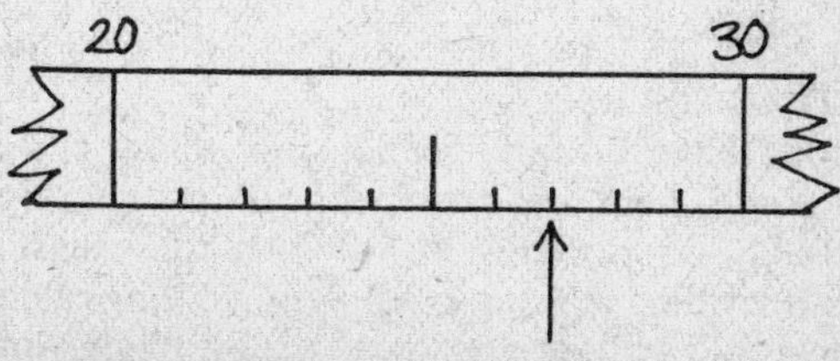

44. Correct measurement of 27.

These are matters where a child needs individual attention and in a class of thirty pupils a child may not receive as much attention as he really needs. From your child's school find which instruments are introduced at what stages and help your child to use and understand them.

Finally, when helping a child, remember that with measurement there are two types of task which may have to be performed. Firstly we may have to measure a particular object, e.g. the length of a line or the weight of a parcel. Alternatively, we may be required to draw a line of given length or weigh out a particular quantity, illustrating the task of constructing something to a given measure. Children need to be able to perform both these types of measurement.

8
SHAPE

Spatial work is a vital part of the mathematics of today's primary school. We live in a three-dimensional world and mathematics arose from our activities in this world. Hence the need to study shapes, both solid (or three-dimensional) and plane (or two-dimensional). Such work features in all school courses, although the coverage varies from school to school. This is because there is no set pattern or accepted body of knowledge which has to be covered as, for example, in calculation. Nevertheless, there are certain ideas which underlie all work on shape and which all children should meet.

The work is aimed to extend the child's experience through handling materials and analysing what is seen. Hence ways in which parents may help mainly consist of supplementing this work. Parents who have memories of their own experiences with geometry in the secondary school may be somewhat surprised by the content and methods. There is no formal geometry, but the work is concerned with figures which are moved about, stretched, enlarged, reduced, reflected, fitted together and so on. The questions that are asked are 'what happens?' and 'why?' as vocabulary and knowledge are extended.

BEGINNINGS

Children's first experiences are of things around them and in the infant school a rich environment is provided for the child to explore, talk and write about. Shapes – natural and man-made – are looked at: flowers, leaves, stones, shells, boxes, etc. They are sorted and classified (see Chapter 4). Shapes are cut out of paper or card and fitted together, sometimes to make plane (i.e. flat) shapes and sometimes to make solids. Patterns are made from simple shapes. Clay and plasticine are made into shapes and then cut up to form more shapes. Wooden bricks are built into shapes and cardboard boxes are cut to form other shapes.

Shapes are observed to be long, thin, tall, round, curved, straight, flat, three-cornered, four-cornered and so on. They may be sorted into sets – triangles, circles, squares, etc. Properties are looked at – edges, corners, faces of solids, solids which roll and those which slide. Shapes are arranged in order of size. The symmetry of shapes is examined.

Drawing takes place; patterns are drawn with straight lines and with circles. Paper is folded and cut out to make patterns. Models are made (houses, castles, windmills) involving different shapes. Throughout there is the beginning of a mathematical vocabulary through words such as cube, circle, triangle, square, etc.

As explained earlier, much of this work can be linked to other work in the infant school. Some of it can lead to calculation and early graphical work in mathematics, but it can also be part of work in language and other fields.

SOME COMMON FIGURES

It is important that the correct names are used when discussing the different figures. Even the very young children seem to enjoy using long names to describe prehistoric monsters and there seems no reason why some of the more difficult names are not used when dealing with the appropriate geometrical shapes.

Of the solid figures, the *sphere, cylinder* and *cube* are so well-known as to need no description. The *pyramid* too, is well-known, especially from the Egyptian pyramids, but these are built on a square base and there are pyramids built on bases of other shapes, e.g. a triangle; if the pyramid has a triangular base, it will only have three triangular faces above that base; this shape is also called a tetrahedron. A brick-shaped object is a cuboid, but is also called a rectangular *prism*. The base – or end on which the brick is standing – is a rectangle, but imagine a similar solid whose base was a triangle; this would be a triangular prism. There are prisms with other shaped bases, e.g. octagonal.

The outer surfaces of solids are called *faces*; thus a cube has six faces which are squares. The faces of a solid meet in lines which are the *edges*, and the edges meet in points which are the *corners* or *vertices* of the solid. A cube has twelve edges and eight vertices.

Plane figures are classified according to the number of sides which they possess. The simplest is a *triangle*; if a triangle has two sides of equal length it is called *isosceles* and if all three sides are equal in length it is called *equilateral*. Four-sided figures are called *quadrilaterals.* If one pair of sides of a quadrilateral is parallel it is a *trapezium.* If both pairs of opposite sides are parallel, it is called a *parallelogram.* If a parallelogram has all its angles equal (i.e. they are right angles), it is a *rectangle*. A parallelogram with all its sides equal is called a *rhombus.* If, however, all the sides are equal and all the angles are equal, the figure is a *square.*

Plane figures with more than four sides are called *polygons*. They can be described by the number of sides, e.g. a five-sided polygon, but the more common ones have their own name. Thus a five-sided polygon is a *pentagon*, one with six sides is a *hexagon*, one with eight sides is an *octagon* and one with ten sides is a *decagon.*

If a figure has all its sides equal and all its angles equal it is said to be *regular*. So a regular pentagon is a five-sided polygon with all its sides equal and all its angles equal. Notice that a regular quadrilateral is a square and a regular triangle is an equilateral triangle.

Children examine other shapes besides those listed above. For example, spirals, ellipses and the circle. At early stages the emphasis is on looking at all shapes and distinguishing particular features.

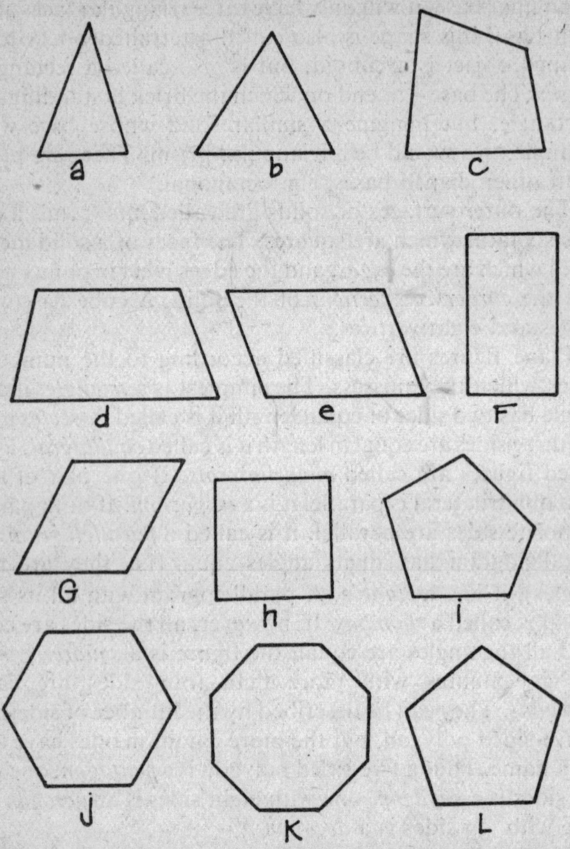

45. a: isosceles triangle, b: equilateral triangle, c: quadrilateral, d: trapezium, e: parallelogram, f: rectangle, g: rhombus, h: square, i: pentagon, j: hexagon, k: octagon, l: regular pentagon.

Two definitions should be noted at this point. The first is that angles represent an amount of turn, as was explained in the last chapter. Secondly, a *line* may be defined as an infinite set of points. Here we are thinking of a line as consisting of a series of points very close together so that they form a continuous line and no matter what the length of the line, an infinite number cán be fitted along it. The correct name for a line of definite length (e.g. 2 cm long) is a *line segment*, the idea being that when we speak of a line generally, we are indicating a line which is of infinite length; that is to say, it extends in each direction indefinitely.

Finally, two ideas of direction are important. If two straight lines meet at right angles, they are *perpendicular*, but if they are the same distance apart, they are said to be *parallel*. The same can be said of planes, of course. Thus two adjacent faces of a cube are at right angles, but two opposite faces of the cube form parallel planes.

The relationship between plane and solid figures is seen when children examine the faces of solids; a cube has faces which are square, a tetrahedron has triangular faces and so on. Solids may also be built up from shapes drawn and cut from a sheet of paper or cardboard. In this case the exercise is to be able to draw the shape which, when cut out and folded, will make a complete solid. The shapes are called the *nets* of the solids and two nets are shown below, for a cube and for a square pyramid.

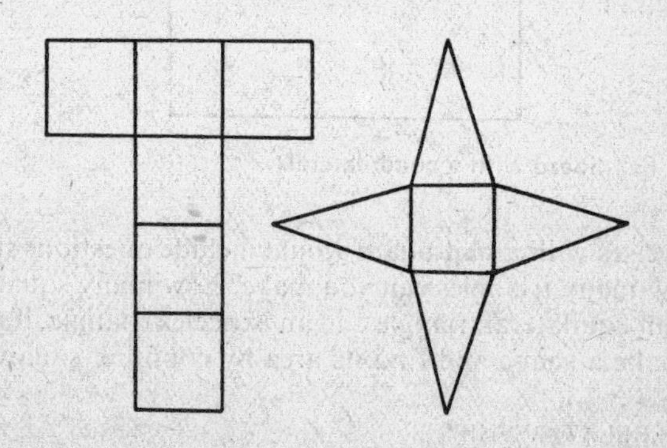

46. The net of a cube (left) and that of a square pyramid (right).

SUGGESTIONS FOR HELP

This is a matter of extending experience. Containers of different sizes and shapes should be collected; shapes examined and faces drawn around; faces, edges and vertices counted. Do they roll (i.e. have curved surfaces) or do they slide?

Paper and cardboard can be cut and folded. Patterns can be drawn and painted.

Milk straws, cocktail sticks or bits of wire can be stuck into small pieces of plasticine to build up solid figures in outline.

A useful aid for work with plane figures is a nail-board. This consists of 9 or 16 short nails in a flat piece of wood, the nails being arranged in a square pattern. Rubber bands can be stretched around the nails to form different shapes. Properties of figures can often be seen from the pattern of nails and ideas of area may also be developed.

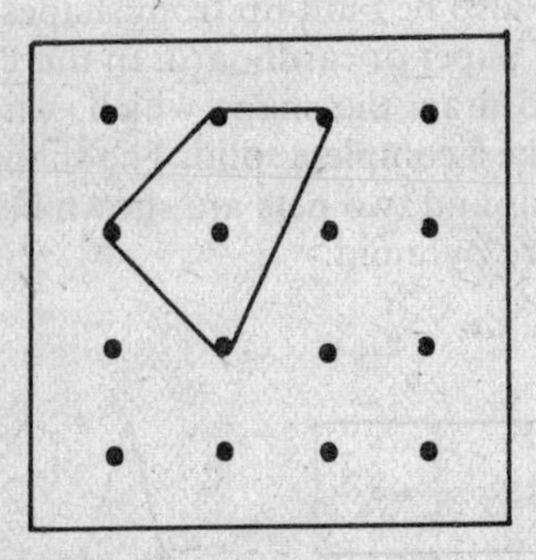

47. A nail-board with a quadrilateral.

Exercises with a nail-board would include questions such as: how many triangles can you make? how many squares? make an equilateral triangle and an isosceles triangle, if you can; make a shape and find its area by counting squares.

ANGLE RELATIONSHIPS

Triangles may be described by the size of their angles. Firstly, the sum of the angles of a triangle is 180° (or two right-angles). This can be demonstrated by cutting a triangle from paper, tearing off the angles and arranging them together, when they will be seen to form a straight line.

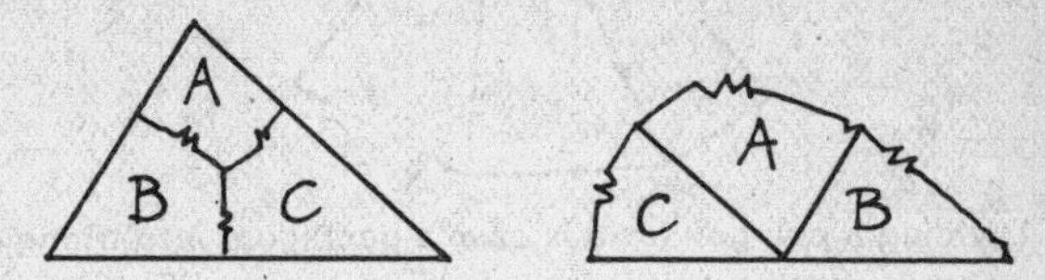

48. The angles of a triangle always add up to 180°.

If the angles of a triangle are each less than a right-angle, it is called an *acute-angled* triangle (Fig. 49(a)); if one angle of the triangle is a right-angle, it is a *right-angled* triangle (b); and if one of the angles of a triangle is greater than 90° (i.e. is an obtuse angle), it is called an *obtuse-angled* triangle (c).

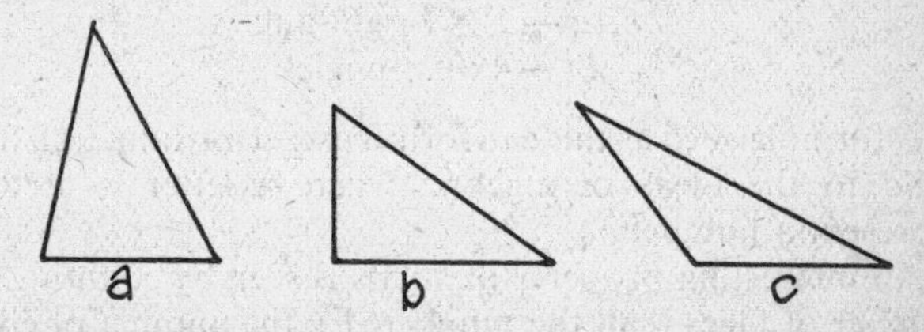

49. (a) acute-angled triangle, (b) right-angled triangle, (c) obtuse-angled triangle.

If from a corner of a quadrilateral or polygon lines are drawn to each of the other corners, the figure is divided into a number of triangles, as shown here:

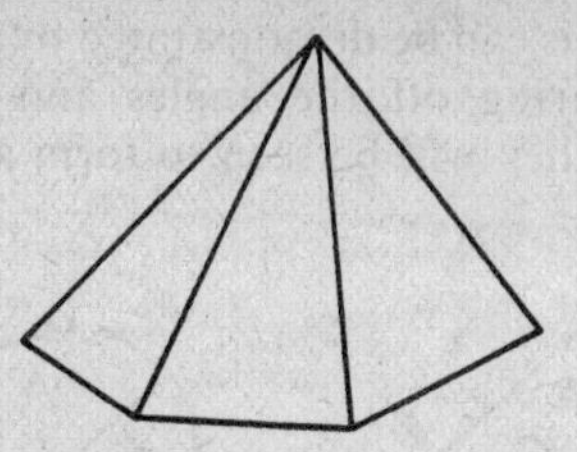

50. Dividing a polygon (in this case a pentagon) into triangles.

The number of triangles formed is always two less than the number of sides of the original figure. Since the sum of the angles of a triangle is two right-angles, we have a means of finding the sum of the angles of any polygon: count the number of sides, subtract 2, double the result, and this gives the equivalent number of right-angles. As an example, for a hexagon (i.e. six sides), the sum of the angles will be equivalent to eight right-angles or 720°. Once the principle has been understood, the explanation of the calculation can be made clearer by the use of a formula. If n is the number of sides of the figure, the sum of the angles is

$$(n - 2) \times 2 \text{ right-angles}$$
or
$$2n - 4 \text{ right-angles.}$$

A formula such as this can form a useful introduction for a child to the ideas of algebra, where a letter is used to represent a number.

An interesting property of solids is seen by counting the number of faces (call the number, F), the number of edges (E), and the number of vertices (V). These are related by the formula

$$V + F - E = 2$$

Taking a cube as an example, $V = 8$, $F = 6$, $E = 12$, so $8 + 6 - 12 = 2$. This is known as Euler's Theorem. Children can demonstrate this for themselves with different solid shapes.

PERIMETER, AREA AND VOLUME

The distance all round a plane figure is called its *perimeter.* The space inside the perimeter is the *area*; this has been dealt with in the chapter on measurement. In the case of a solid figure, the amount of material in it is its *volume*, which was also dealt with in the earlier chapter. An important idea relating to measurement in spatial work is that of *scale.*

Ideas of scale come from scale drawings, plans and maps. The basic idea is one which is fundamental to mathematics, i.e. proportion. This topic will be developed in the next two chapters, but for the moment it will be considered in relation to scale. If we have a plan of a room or building on which a length of 1 cm represents a length of 1 metre on the actual room or building, then we know that a distance of 2 cm on the plan represents 2 metres, 3 cm on the plan represents 3 metres and so on. The plan and the building are in proportion. Since a length on the building is 100 times the corresponding length on the plan, we can say that there is a *scale factor* of 100 in this particular case. This means that to find the real-life distance, we multiply the corresponding distance on the plan by 100.

What happens to the area or the volume in such cases? A simple diagram will illustrate. Suppose we have a square (shaded in the diagram) whose side is of length 1 unit, e.g.

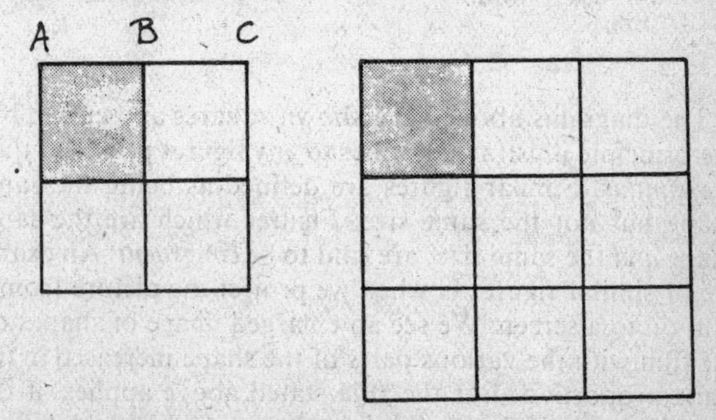

51. What happens to the area when the length of the side is multiplied by two, and by three.

AB. Double this length as shown at AC and this is the side of the new square. This new square is four times the area of the original square. The second diagram shows that if we treble the length, we multiply the area by 9.

Clearly, multiplying the length by 4, the area would be multiplied by 16 and so on, i.e. if the length is multiplied by n, then the area is multiplied by n^2. This idea is not always appreciated by adults, let alone children! Turning to volume, the diagram below shows that doubling a length multiplies the volume by 8. Trebling it will multiply the volume by 27. Or generally, if a length is multiplied by n, the volume is multiplied by n^3.

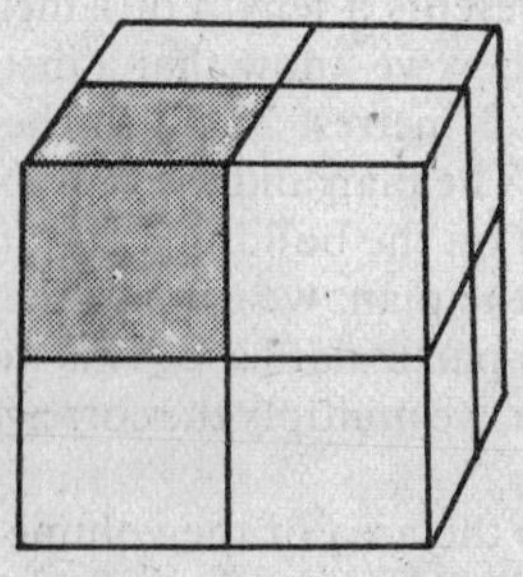

52. What happens to the volume when the length of each side of a cube is doubled.

The diagrams above have shown squares and cubes, but the principle illustrated applies to any figures provided they are *similar*. Similar figures are defined as being the same shape but not the same size. Figures which are the same shape *and* the same size, are said to be *congruent*. An example of similar figures is when we project the picture from a film on to a screen. We see an enlarged image of shapes on the film with the various parts of the shape increased in the same proportion. But the rule stated above applies: if the magnification of the image on to the screen enlarges a length n times, then any area will be enlarged n^2 times.

In the case of solid figures, an example is when some winner of a trophy only holds the trophy for a year but is given a small replica to keep. Provided that the replica is an exact copy of the original, the volume of the original will be n^3 times the volume of the replica, where n is the number of times greater of corresponding lengths. For example, suppose the replica is 10 cm high and the original trophy is 40 cm high, then the volume of the trophy is 64 times (i.e. 4^3) the volume of the replica. Since weight of a solid object depends on volume, the weight of the trophy will be 64 times the weight of the replica. Also if the trophy is in the form of a cup which will hold a certain quantity of champagne, the replica will hold only $\frac{1}{64}$th of that amount.

Parents may be able to get children to do some interesting calculations based on scale models, such as toy motor cars, dolls, etc.

THE CIRCLE

The circle occupies a special position among the plane figures which children meet. Various terms are used in the work, the *circumference* being the distance round the circle (its perimeter), the *diameter* is the total distance across passing through the centre, and half that distance is the

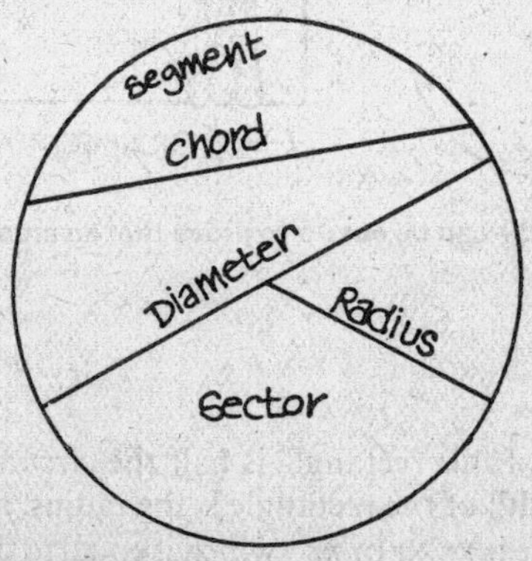

53. Aspects of a circle.

radius. A line joining two points on the circumference is called a *chord* and this line divides the circle into two *segments*. Children will meet some or all of these terms, but the most important are radius and circumference.

The circumference of a circle is always a constant number of times the length of the diameter. This number is an irrational number, i.e. its exact value cannot be found. This value is denoted by the Greek letter pi, written π. When doing calculations it is left to the individual to use a value of π which is sufficiently accurate for his purposes. A common decimal approximation is 3·142. Children often do measuring exercises with jars, cylindrical tins, etc. to show that the circumference is a certain number of times the diameter and find approximate values for this constant.

Some older children may proceed to find the formula for the area of a circle. Since the diameter is twice the radius, the length of the circumference can be written as $2\pi r$, where r is the radius. Imagine the circle cut into a large number of small sectors and these re-arranged in alternate directions to form a rectangle approximately.

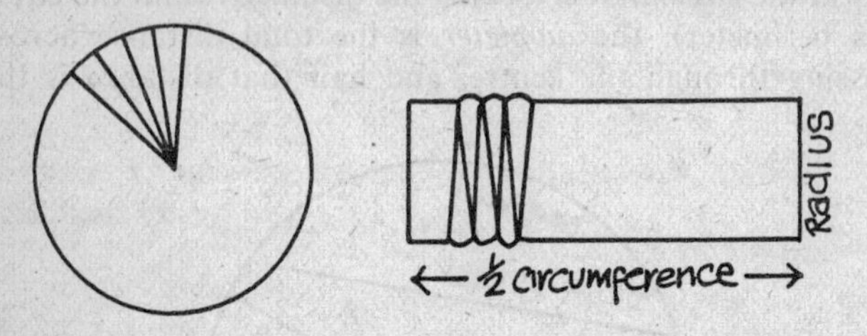

54. How a circle can be cut up to prove that an area is πr^2.

The length of this rectangle is half the circumference, i.e. πr, and the width of the rectangle is the radius, r. So the area of the rectangle is $\pi r \times r$ or πr^2, which is equal to the area of the circle.

REFLECTIONS, ROTATIONS AND TRANSLATIONS

Much of the work on shape which is done in schools is concerned with the results of handling and moving shapes. Children can do much of the early work by using plastic or cardboard plane shapes around which they can draw. One of the simplest movements is to slide the shape to a new position; this is a *translation.* The new figure is exactly the same shape and size as the old and the corresponding sides are parallel.

55. A triangle is translated (slid).

Instead of sliding, the shape could be rotated about some point, which may be inside or outside the figure. Once more the new shape is the same size and shape as the old, but the corresponding sides of the two figures are no longer parallel. This movement is a *rotation.*

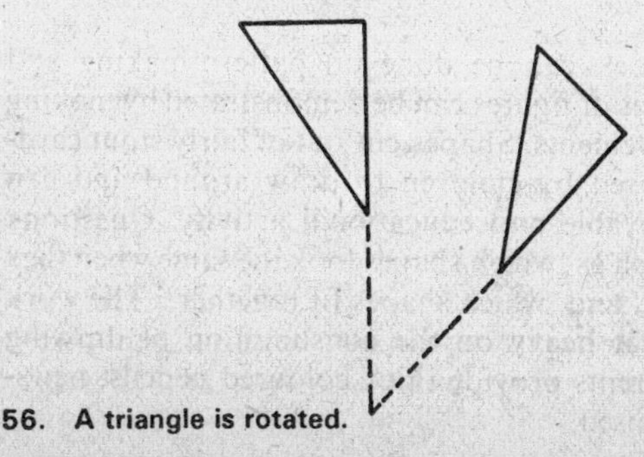

56. A triangle is rotated.

Finally, imagine the figure reflected in a mirror. The two figures are the same shape and size but the effect has been as though the figure was cut from card and turned over. A *reflection* of this nature has to be done about a line and if this line coincides with one of the sides of the figure, a symmetrical shape is produced by combining the original and new figures.

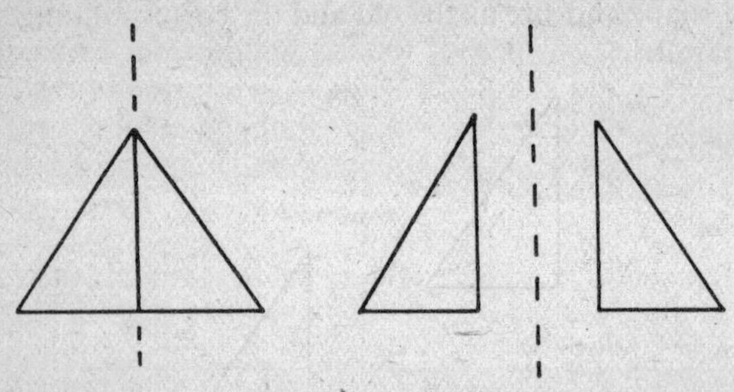

57. Triangles can be reflected. The left-hand one is reflected about one of the sides, and symmetry is produced by combining the new with the old.

Of course, it is possible to combine the various movements. For example, we may reflect a figure in a line and then rotate the reflected figure about some point. Or we may reflect a figure in a line, then reflect the new figure in another line.

Interesting work can be done on pattern-making and various properties of figures can be demonstrated by making use of these movements. Shapes cut out of fairly stout cardboard can be used by children to draw around and can provide an enjoyable and educational activity. Questions can be asked, such as 'which shapes look the same when they are turned over?' and 'which shapes fit together?' The work can be somewhat heavy on the consumption of drawing paper, but if parents provide thick coloured pencils, newspaper could be used.

TESSELLATIONS

The work just described leads directly to two of the newer topics widely introduced into the primary school: tessellations and symmetry. The first of these is concerned with tiling patterns and finding which shapes will cover a plane surface completely. Children experiment by drawing round different shapes. The diagram below shows a pattern made from triangles. Starting from any one triangle, it is a useful exercise to say which of the adjoining triangles has been obtained by translation, reflection or rotation of the initial triangle. But the figure also contains parallelograms and hexagons, showing that these two shapes will also tessellate a plane surface.

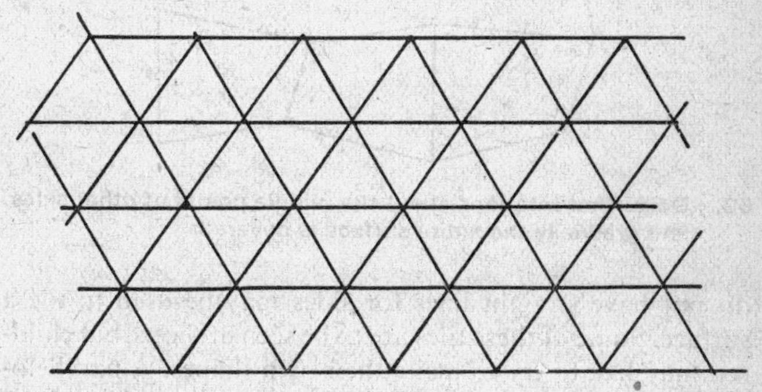

58. A tiling pattern made from triangles.

Can we use quadrilateral shaped tiles (see (A) below) to cover a surface? At first this does not seem likely. But rotate the figure about the middle point of one of the sides; P in figure (B) below.

We may do further rotations about the middle points of other sides of the quadrilateral, so that gradually the entire surface is covered.

Further questions can be asked. Will pentagons tessellate a surface? Will octagons? And finally, what is it which determines whether these things are possible? Also figures which

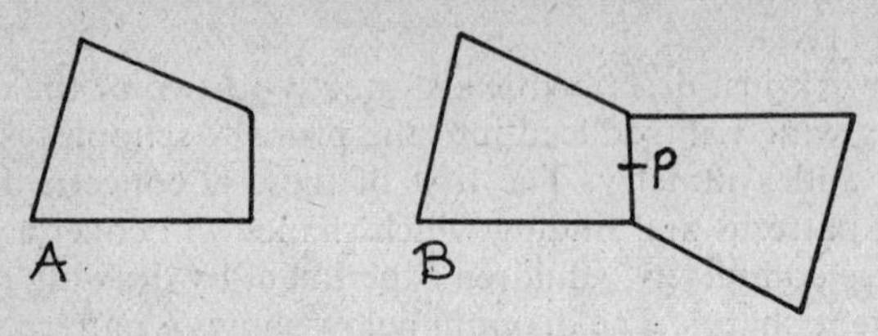

59. Rotate the quadrilateral about the middle point of one of its sides.

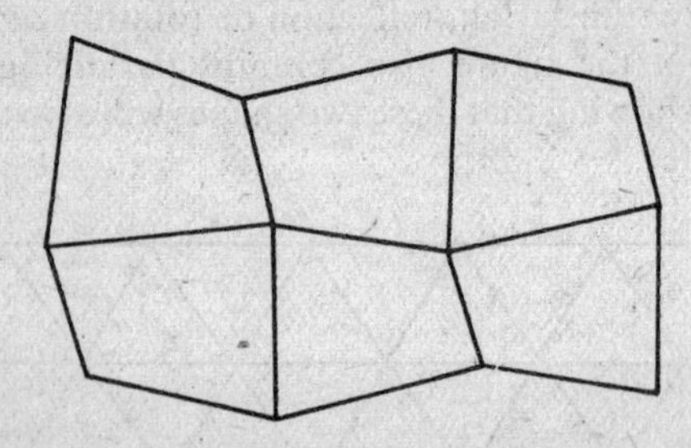

60. Do further rotations about the middle points of other sides, and gradually the entire surface is covered.

do not have straight lines for sides may be used to tile a surface. Some of these tiles are to be seen in shops, but children may like to try to make their own shapes. A parallelogram or rhombus may be used for a starting grid and the shape of each side changed so that when the figure is rotated about the middle point of the side, it fits (see (A) below). It will be seen that one half of the new side is the shape of the other half rotated through two right-angles. Patterns can be developed as shown in (B) below. The artist M. C. Escher has produced some interesting pictures using these methods.[1]

SYMMETRY

The simplest form of symmetry is where a figure is reflected about the line containing one of its sides; this line is called the axis of *symmetry*. (See (A) below.) If the figure is cut from

1. M. C. Escher: Graphic Work. Macdonald.

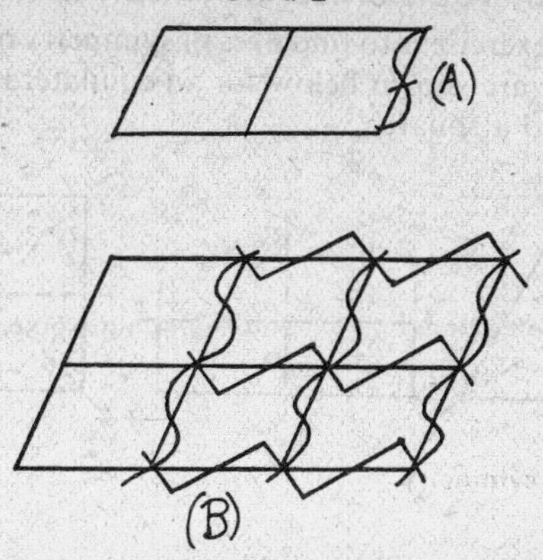

61. How the surface may be tiled with shapes which do not have straight sides.

paper and then folded along the axis of symmetry, the two halves fit exactly. Children cut symmetrical shapes from folded paper in this way. However, if a folded sheet is folded again with the second fold at right-angles to the first, the resultant cut-out figure will have two axes of symmetry (see (B) below).

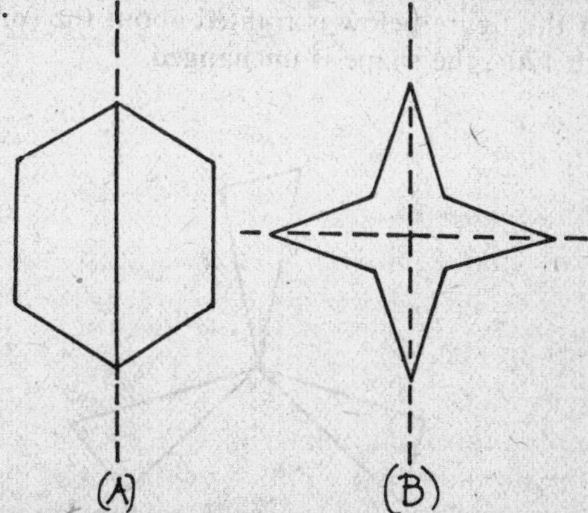

62. (a) Symmetry; the axis of symmetry, (b) a figure with two axes of symmetry.

A pupil's exercise is to find axes of symmetry of particular figures; they are shown below for an equilateral triangle, a rectangle and a square.

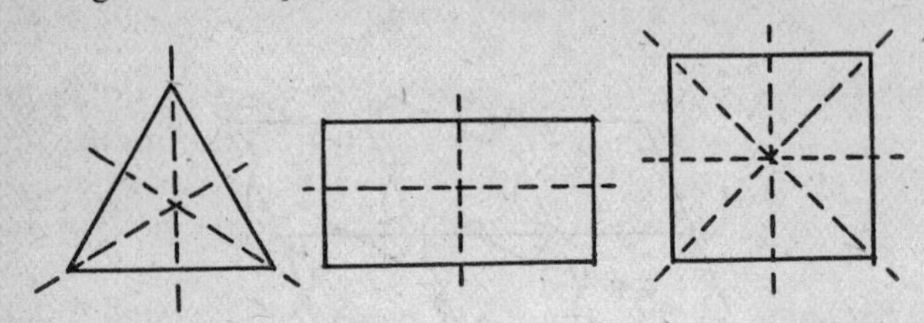

63. Axes of symmetry.

An interesting exercise is for a pupil to take the alphabet in capital letters and decide which letters have one or more axes of symmetry.

The type of symmetry so far described is known as line *symmetry*, since there is symmetry about a line. However there is also *rotational symmetry*. This is obtained when a figure is rotated about some point and the shape in the new position is exactly the same as the shape in the initial position. If the figure below is rotated about the central point through 120°, the shape is unchanged.

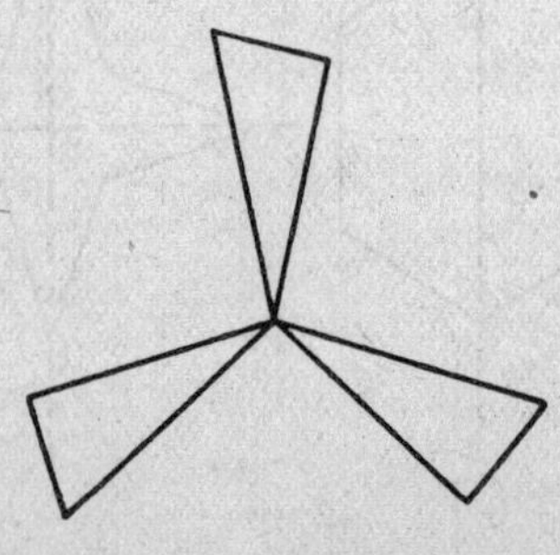

64. Rotational symmetry. The shape is exactly the same when rotated about the central point through 120°.

It is possible, of course, for a figure to have both rotational symmetry and line symmetry. An equilateral triangle is an example. When rotated about a central point through 120°, it displays rotational symmetry; it also has three axes of symmetry as was shown above (Fig. 63).

A particular case of rotational symmetry is *point symmetry*. This is when a figure may be rotated through an angle of 180° to display the same shape and position as before (see (A) below). It will be seen that this type of symmetry applies to the tiling shown in Fig. 61. The shape in (B) below looks exactly the same when it is rotated about the central point through 90° and also when rotated through 180°, and so displays both rotational and point symmetry.

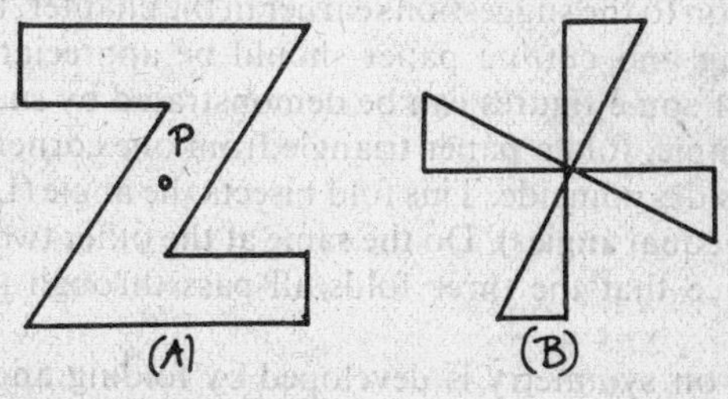

65. Point symmetry.

The symmetry of solid shapes is another aspect of the work but needs to be illustrated by solid models. Some schools may touch on this topic. An application of this is in the study of crystals, a branch of chemistry, and something which a keen child may find to be of interest and worth pursuing on his own. All such interest is to be encouraged and any child undertaking individual work on a topic could be encouraged to write an account of his discoveries. Schools often have displays of 'books' of this nature, which have been produced by pupils.

This outline of work which is included under the general topic of 'Shape' was intended to give parents an idea of the development of the subject. The actual development in the school will extend over a long period; for example, young infant children may first experience symmetry in patterns they look at or with ink-blots in folded paper, and yet some of the other ideas on symmetry described above may not be met until the pupil is in the top junior class. Also it must be remembered that work on shape does not stand alone as a topic but is integrated with other work in mathematics. It can be a source of work on calculation and it has close links with graphical work. Mathematics looks for relationships and this aspect of spatial work needs emphasis.

SUGGESTIONS FOR HELP

In addition to the suggestions earlier in the chapter, the value of folding and cutting paper should be appreciated. Properties of some figures can be demonstrated by such work. For example, fold a paper triangle from one corner, so that the two sides coincide. This fold bisects the angle (i.e. cuts it into two equal angles). Do the same at the other two corners and notice that the three folds all pass through the same point.

Work on symmetry is developed by folding and cutting paper as explained earlier. There are many possibilities for this type of work and in many cases it can be regarded as an interesting play activity.

9
GRAPHICAL WORK

On many occasions in earlier chapters stress has been placed on the value of practical work in mathematics to help understanding and bring meaning to a child's mathematical studies. One important way of representing a problem practically is by the use of a graph. Graphs show relationships and it is the search for relationship which lies at the very heart of mathematics. It follows that graphs should be used throughout a mathematics course, sometimes to illustrate the work and aid understanding and at other times as a means of solving a problem. The work described in this chapter would extend throughout the primary school course, being used at appropriate points and being integrated with other work.

It must be admitted that not all teachers make the fullest use of graphical work in their teaching, so that some of the work described here may not be covered in some schools. Nevertheless, parents would be well advised to note carefully these ideas, since sometimes drawing an appropriate graph may help a child who is having difficulty with a problem. A graph shows its message clearly, whereas a mass of mathematical symbols can create confusion. Think, for example, of the way in which mathematical statistics (e.g. a country's exports or a firm's output) become much more understandable when set out as a graph.

Early graphical work in schools is of two types. The first is the arrow diagram to show relationships; these were described in Chapter 4. The more formal type of graph is usually introduced with simple representation of statistics. As described in the chapter on 'Early Work', children would fasten squares of coloured paper on to a sheet to represent that they had a dog, a cat, or other pet and gradually a column graph would be built up. The next step would be to first count the numbers of different pets owned by the children. From this information columns of appropriate lengths can be drawn without the need to stick on individual squares.

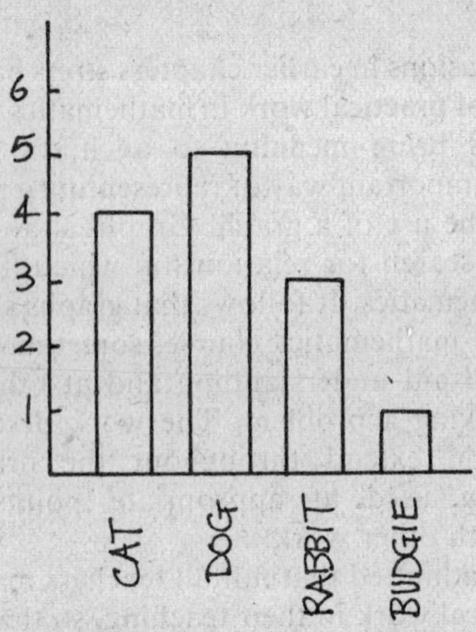

66. Pet popularity graph.

This type of graph is used for the recording of other information, e.g. heights of pupils in the class, or numbers who come to school by car, by bus, walking, etc. *Column graphs* of this type are used throughout the school at different stages and, later, such a graph may be used to introduce the idea of an average or mean. Suppose each column represents the amount of pocket money which each child receives.

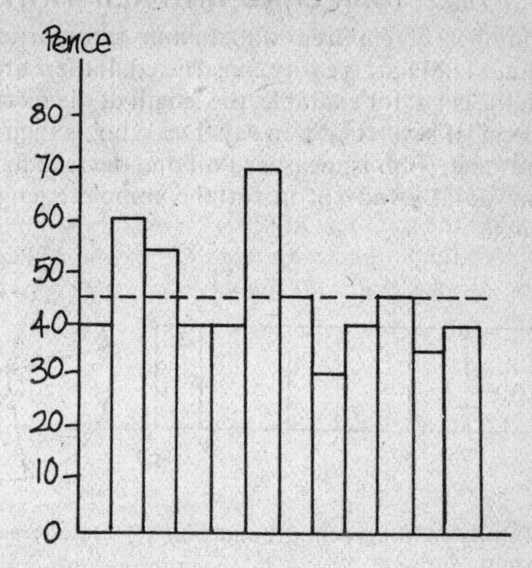

67. Pocket money graph.

Imagine that the entire graph was levelled by raising the smaller columns with lengths from the taller columns, very much in the way that a bulldozer levels a patch of ground. The total length of all the original columns represents the total amount of spending money which the children receive and this has now been re-distributed so that each child has the same amount. This is shown in the broken line on the graph above and represents the average amount of spending money which the children receive.

BLOCK GRAPHS AND PIE CHARTS

The column graphs illustrated above are sometimes called *block graphs*, but this term may also be applied to a different type of representation. If the children in a class had been asked to state their favourite TV programme, the information could be shown as parts of a rectangle which are divided off in such a way that the area of each part is proportional to the number of children who favour that particular programme. The chart is easily constructed. If there are 30 children in the class, for example, the length of the rectangle may be 30 cm. If seven children say 'Dr. Who' is their favourite programme, 7 cm is measured off and the rectangle divided at this point. And so on for the complete length of the rectangle.

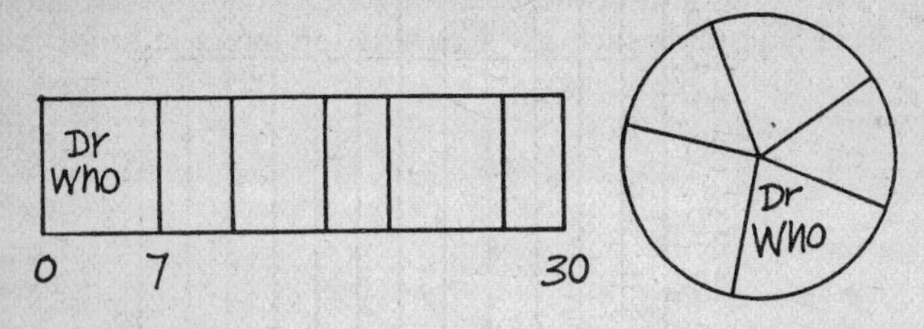

68. Television programme popularity (a) block graph, (b) pie chart.

A variation of this is the *pie chart* where a circle is divided proportionally to the various statistics. Taking the same example, the circle would be divided firstly by marking off $\frac{7}{30}$ths to represent the Dr. Who enthusiasts. Since the angle at the centre of the circle is 360°, then 12° will represent one child, so we measure off an angle of 84° (i.e. 7×12) and draw a sector which represents these children.

There can be a difficulty with this type of diagram if 360° does not divide easily by the fractional parts. For example, if there had been 29 children in the class, one child would be represented by an angle of $\frac{360}{29}$°, which is neither easy to calculate nor to measure.

POINTS ON A PLANE

Returning to the column graphs described above, notice that, whereas the vertical columns are marked off by the line of the vertical scale which they reach, each column is represented horizontally by a space between two lines. The next type of graph which we shall consider depends on fixing the position of a point on a piece of paper (i.e. on a plane) by finding the intersection of two lines. The difference needs to be stressed because sometimes children experience difficulty over this change.

Some teachers introduce the new idea by making reference to the American pattern of towns with roads running at right-angles to each other, the roads in one direction being called streets and in the other direction are called avenues. Hence questions such as 'Where is the intersection of 5th Street and 3rd Avenue?'

On graphs, axes are marked off in units in each direction and a point is represented by a *number pair*, e.g. (3,5). This is an *ordered pair* of numbers where each number represents a distance along one axis; an ordered pair means that the order in which we write the numbers matters. Ordered pairs are used in many different situations in mathematics – see Chapter 11. In graphical work, it is usually understood that the first number of a pair represents the distance on the horizontal axis and the second number, the distance on the vertical axis. These two distances are called the *co-ordinates* of the point. Where the two lines from the axes meet is the required point and it can be seen from the diagram below

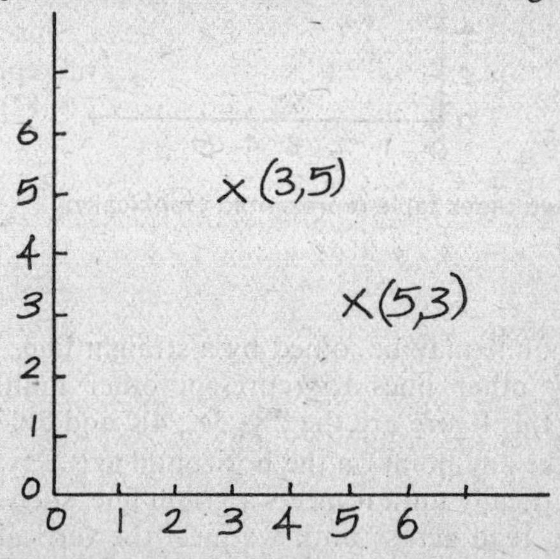

69. Co-ordinates: position 5,3 is not the same as 3,5.

that, for example, the point (5,3) is not the same as the point (3,5).

If algebraic notation is being used, we refer to the horizontal axis as the x-axis and the vertical axis as the y-axis, so that a number pair such as (3,5) means that $x = 3$ and $y = 5$, and these are often called the x — co-ordinate and the y — co-ordinate. Sometimes the number pair is referred to as the *address* of that particular point, since it fixes its position.

We may write a series of number pairs according to a particular rule or relationship. For example these:

(1,2), (2,4), (3,6), (4,8), (5,10), (6,12)

are such that the second number is twice the first. If these points are plotted on a graph, they represent the 2-times multiplication table.

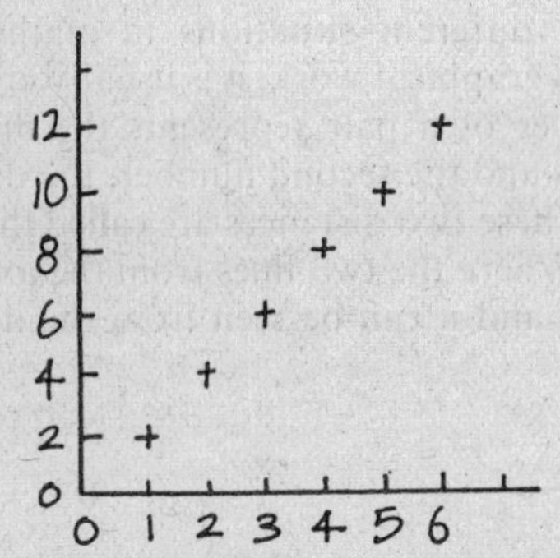

70. The two times table represented graphically.

These points may be joined by a straight line. We could also draw other lines to represent other multiplication tables. In this figure are the 2×, 3×, 4× and 5× tables.

If we take any point on the horizontal axis, say 4, follow the line vertically until it meets a graph line, such as the 3× table, then read across until we meet the vertical axis, we obtain the multiple of our original number, in this case 12

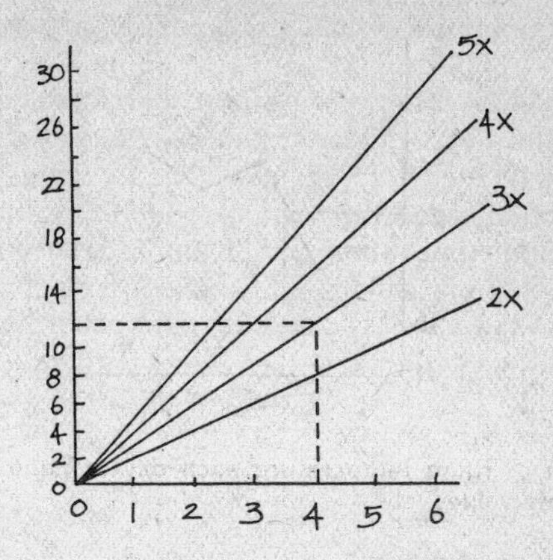

71. The two, three, four and five times table represented graphically.

(see the broken line above). It is possible to use the graph to read off intermediate values. Thus, repeating the above, but starting at the point representing $4\frac{1}{2}$ instead of 4, we obtain an answer of $13\frac{1}{2}$, which is $3 \times 4\frac{1}{2}$.

This ability to read off from the graph, values which lie between those values which have been plotted, only applies in cases where the relationship shown in the graph is a continuous one. That is to say that at all times, if one of the quantities represented on one axis changes, there is a corresponding change in the quantity represented on the other axis.

The alternative case is where there is no means of knowing what relationship there is between the two quantities for points between those actually plotted. Suppose on a graph are plotted the temperatures in a room at noon each day from Monday to Friday. These are shown in the diagram below and the points have been joined by straight lines.

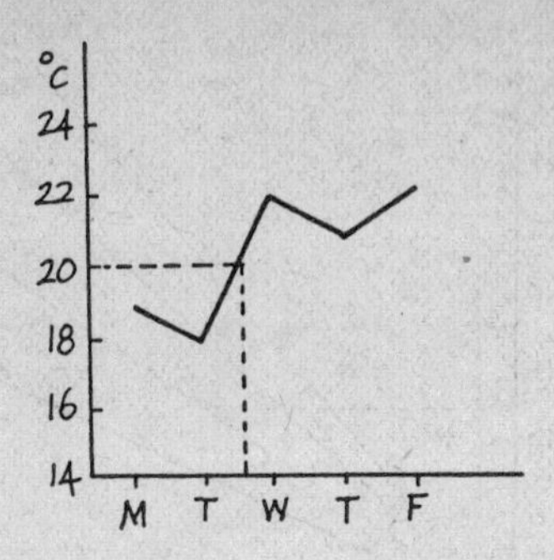

72. Graph of room temperature each day at noon. These are discrete values.

From the graph it will be seen that the temperature on Tuesday noon was 18°C and on Wednesday noon was 22°C. Halfway between these two times is midnight of Tuesday/Wednesday. Taking this point on the horizontal axis, reading up to the graph and on to the other axis, we find the corresponding temperature of 20°C. Was this the temperature in the room at midnight? Clearly we cannot use this graph in this way. The values displayed are only true for those points plotted; points which lie between have no meaning. These values are called *discrete* as opposed to the continuous variables of the multiplication graphs.

It is incorrect, therefore, to connect the plotted points by lines in this case; they should remain as unique points. The correct method of display in such cases is to drop perpendicular lines from each of the points on to the horizontal axis as shown below:

READING A GRAPH

When children draw graphs, it is important that they discuss what the graph shows, explain, or try to find reasons for, any significant feature of the graph (e.g. a sudden rise or fall) and try to draw some conclusion. Since a graph shows a relation-

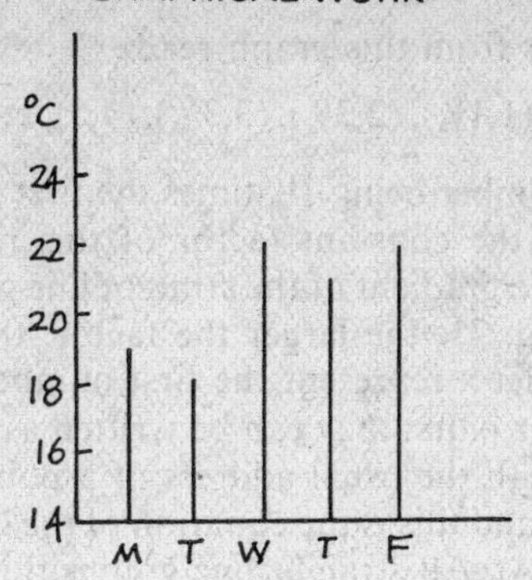

73. The correct way to display discrete variables.

ship between certain things, it can help us to understand better that particular relationship.

The straight line graphs of the multiplication tables in Fig. 71 indicate a relation between the two sets which is known as *direct proportion*. As the numbers in one set increase, those in the other set increase correspondingly. This is a common form of relationship met in many everyday situations, e.g. the cost of many materials. If certain material costs £1.25 per kilogramme, a price graph can be drawn as shown:

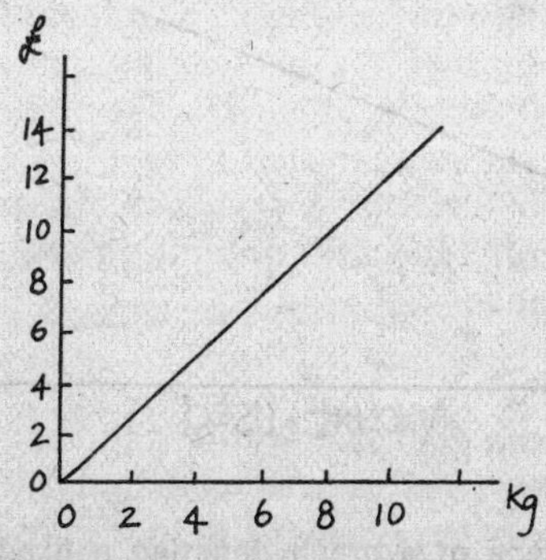

74. Graph of material costing £1.25 per kg.

Number pairs from this graph read:

$$(1,1\tfrac{1}{4}), (2,2\tfrac{1}{2}), (3,3\tfrac{3}{4}), (4,5), \text{etc.},$$

the second number being $1\frac{1}{4}$ times the first number of each pair. This is the constant factor of this relationship and determines the gradient of the straight line graph. As can be seen from Fig. 71, the larger the factor, the steeper is the graph. If we let x represent the first number of each of the above number pairs, they can be written as $(x, 1\frac{1}{4}x)$. Comparing this with the usual address of a point, (x,y), we see that $y = 1\frac{1}{4}x$ and this is the equation of the line on the graph above (Fig. 74). All straight line graphs through the origin (i.e. the point $(0,0)$) have an equation of the form $y = mx$, where m represents the gradient of the line.

The cost of some things is based on a fixed charge together with a charge depending on the amount bought. Examples are gas and electricity, where the bills show a fixed charge together with a charge per therm or unit used, and taxi charges which consist of a fixed amount plus a charge per mile. A graph of such examples is of this form:

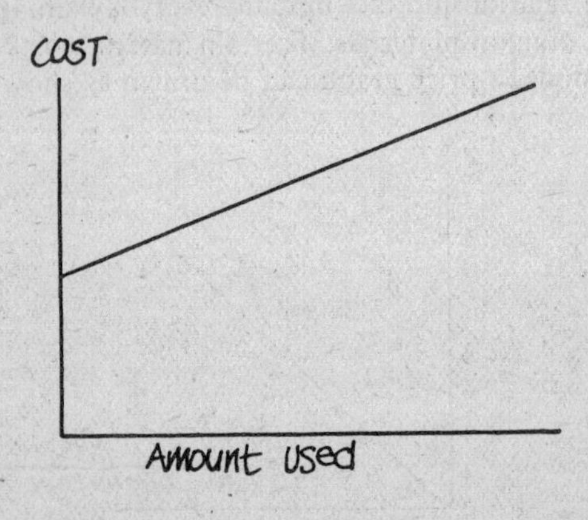

75. Typical shape of a graph denoting a fixed charge plus a charge for units used.

This is similar to the last graph, the line being steeper the higher the charge, but now the line does not pass through the origin. Instead it cuts the vertical axis at a point corresponding to the fixed charge; this is clearly so, because if, for example, no electricity is used, this fixed charge has to be paid.

A simple example of number pairs which would give such a graph is:

(0,2), (1,3), (2,4), (3,5), (4,6), . . .

where in each pair the second number is 2 more than the first. Children can make up sets of number pairs using rules such as the above and then plot these on to graph paper to see the results. Sometimes the results are straight lines which are in a different direction to the previous examples. Such an instance is where the sum of the numbers in each pair adds up to 10. This gives a set of pairs which starts:

(10,0), (9,1), (8,2), (7,3), . . .

and the graph is:

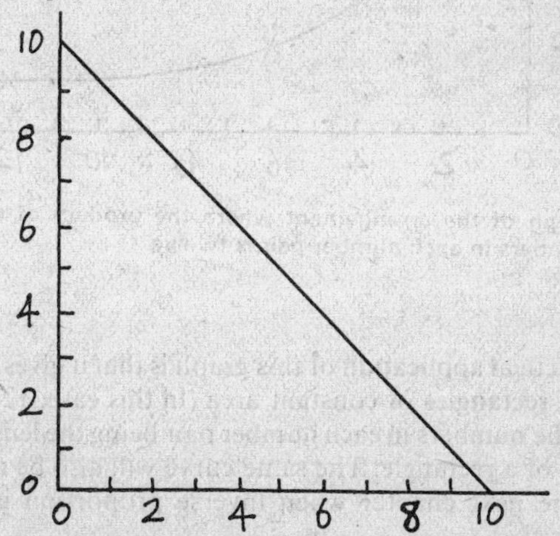

76. Graph of the arrangement whereby the two numbers in each number pair add up to ten.

Graphs are not always straight lines. If we take number pairs where the product of the numbers in each pair is 12, we have:

$$(12,1), (6,2), (4,3), (3,4), \ldots$$

and the graph is as follows:

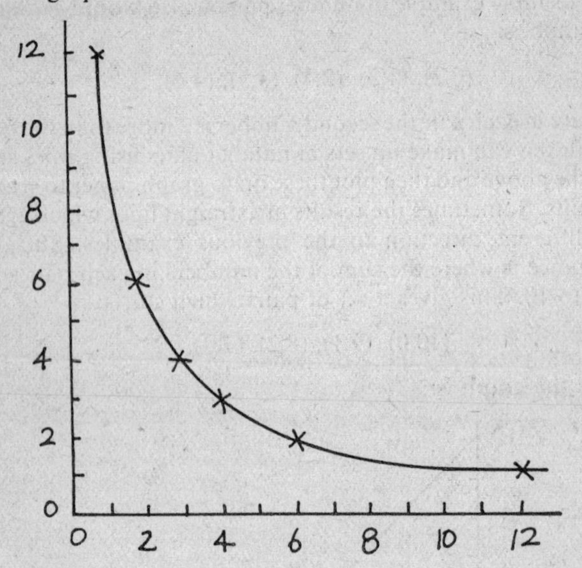

77. Graph of the arrangement where the product of the two numbers in each number pair is twelve.

A practical application of this graph is that it gives dimensions of rectangles of constant area (in this case, 12 square units), the numbers in each number pair being the length and breadth of a rectangle. The same curve will also be referred to in the next chapter when inverse proportion is being considered.

It was pointed out earlier that graphical work runs throughout the mathematics course and graphs can be used in conjunction with many topics which have appeared earlier in the book. The last example may be introduced when rectangles are being considered under the heading of shape. Another instance is when dealing with equivalent fractions; see Chapter 6. A fraction may be written as an ordered pair of numbers with the denominator as the first number and the numerator as the second. Thus the equivalent fractions:

$$\frac{2}{3}, \frac{4}{6}, \frac{6}{9}, \frac{8}{12}, \frac{10}{15}, \text{etc.}$$

may be written as

$$(3,2), (6,4), (9,6), (12,8), (15,10), \text{etc.}$$

Plot these on a graph; the denominators will be on the horizontal axis and the numerators on the vertical one. The points representing the fractions form a straight line; it is possible to have intermediate values, so we may draw the line.

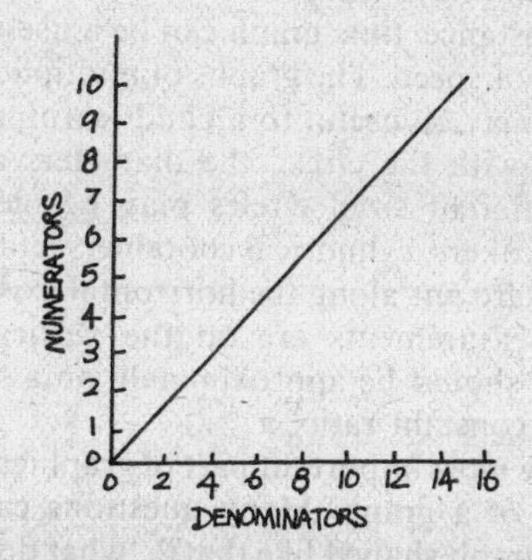

78. Graph of equivalent fractions.

Now read off, from this line, any fractions which are equivalent to those given. A fraction which is represented by a point *not* on the line, e.g. (5,3) or $\frac{3}{5}$, is *not* equivalent to those given. Other sets of equivalent fractions will lie on other lines, of course, so that $\frac{3}{5}$ will lie on the line passing through the points (5,3), (10,6), (15,9), etc.

There are other types of graph which may be introduced into the primary course, but those given above are the most commonly used and the principles that have been explained here apply generally.

SUGGESTIONS FOR HELP

It is unlikely that children will need much in the way of parental help in drawing graphs since the principles are fairly simple. Plain paper may be used if care is taken in drawing and graduating the axes, but square-ruled paper may be purchased from most large stationers. The two main areas in which parents may be able to help with graphical work are (a) by the use of graphs to illustrate other work, and (b) in interpreting graphs.

It has been pointed out already that a graph can often help in the understanding of a problem. Thus in Chapter 7 it was stated that a distance/time graph can be a useful aid to the understanding of speed. The graphs of multiplication tables shown earlier may be useful to a child learning the tables. When dealing with the circle, the diameters and circumferences of different sized circles may be measured (use circular tins, beakers, cylindrical containers, etc.). Diameter measurements are put along the horizontal axis and the circumference measurements are on the vertical axis. The points plotted should lie approximately on a straight line, indicating the constant ratio, π.

Probably the most important part of graphical work is the interpretation of a graph. Many questions can be asked: 'why was the graph shaped like that?', 'what does the graph show?', and even 'has this graph been drawn satisfactorily?'. In the case of a straight line graph showing the cost of certain material, we may ask 'why is it a straight line?' and expect some answer explaining that this is because of equal increases for equal amounts added on; some children may explain it in terms of equal steps up the graph. With statistical graphs, the shape should be looked at and 'kinks' explained. A graph of the ways in which children in a particular school travel to school may show that more children walk than travel by other means; why is this?

Graphs often appear in newspapers, magazines and promotional literature and are usually employed to convey a particular message. Often a graph is drawn incorrectly in order to emphasize the point being made. Children should be encouraged to look at published graphs, to discuss and interpret them, and to spot incorrect practice. With increased use of statistical information in everyday life, this is an important part of general education.

SOME DIFFICULTIES IN GRAPHICAL WORK

Children often have difficulty in choosing an appropriate scale for a graph, i.e. how the figures shall be spaced out on the axes. Sometimes this results in the graph running off the edge of the paper, at other times a very small graph is tucked into a corner of a large sheet. Most graphs drawn by young children which have numbered axes, will start the numbering from zero, so before putting numbers on the sheet, the child needs to think whether all the required numbers are going to fit on. In practice, not all graphs need to start from zero on the vertical axis, but with column graphs it is essential that they do. The columns have to be proportional in height, so that a column representing 40, say, has to be twice the height of a column representing 20. This will only be true if the vertical axis starts from zero.

Some older pupils may meet statistical graphs involving what are known as *class intervals*. Suppose a graph is drawn to show the number of pupils in a school who are aged 7 to 8, 8 to 9, 9 to 10, and 10 to 11. If a child is exactly 8 on the day of the survey, does he go into the first group or the second? A way around this difficulty is to use a minus sign after the 8, thus 8^-, to denote children up to, but not including, the age of 8. So a *frequency table* is prepared showing the number of children in each group:

Intervals	*Frequency*
$7 - 8^-$	34
$8 - 9^-$	27
$9 - 10^-$	31
$10 - 11^-$	29

and the graph is drawn:

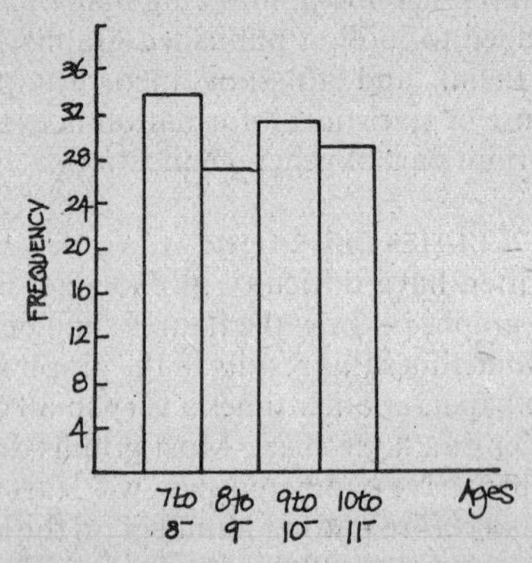

79. Frequency table showing number of children in each age group.

10
THE SEARCH FOR PATTERN

Pattern, in whatever form, implies relationship and the search for relationship is one of the fundamental processes of mathematical thought. So, in children's education, we encourage them to look for pattern.

A child seeing a pattern in coloured rods – a yellow rod, a red rod, a yellow, a red, etc. – becomes aware of the alternating sequence and is able to predict the next in the series. Very young children see patterns and are asked to continue them or they are encouraged to make up their own patterns through activities like threading coloured beads on to a string. They are asked to look for patterns in their surroundings – on wallpapers, in dress materials, in floor tilings, in pottery, etc. Similarly they build up patterns using lino cuts or potato cuts to print their own designs. This develops, in time, to an appreciation of the different types of geometrical transformation – rotation, reflection, translation and enlargement or reduction.

Work develops similarly on pattern in number. Firstly comes the representation of numbers in patterns. For example, five may be shown in various ways, e.g.:

```
o o   o o   o o o o   o o   o o o o o
 o    o o         o   o
o o     o             o o
```

Patterns are seen in sequences of numbers. Counting on in twos, threes, etc. is an early example. At a later stage, sequences of numbers are given and children are asked to continue the pattern, e.g.:

2, 5, 8, 11, . . ., . . .
1, 2, 4, 7, 11, . . ., . . .
2, 6, 18, 54, . . ., . . .

Patterns may also be seen on the 100-square by shading multiples of numbers, e.g. multiples of 3:

1	2	3	4	5	6	7	8	9	10
11	12	13	14	15	16	17	18	19	20
21	22	23	24	25	26	27	28	29	30
31	32	33	34	35	36	37	38	39	40
41	42	43	44	45	46	47	48	49	50
51	52	53	54	55	56	57	58	59	60
61	62	63	64	65	66	67	68	69	70
71	72	73	74	75	76	77	78	79	80
81	82	83	84	85	86	87	88	89	90
91	92	93	94	95	96	97	98	99	100

80. Shading out the numbers which are multiples of three.

The sense of pattern, too, develops with operations on number. For example the fact that $3 + 4 = 7$ relates to $13 + 4 = 17$, $23 + 4 = 27$, etc., and to $30 + 40 = 70$, $300 + 400 = 700$, etc. It is important that children appreciate such facts and the appeal to pattern can help in memorization.

Many patterns, both spatial and numerical, occur in everyday life and parents can help at this stage by making children aware of these patterns, encouraging them to look for them and to analyse them.

RELATIONS

It will be seen that the idea of a relation underlies many of the topics already covered in this book. The relation of one-to-one correspondence between the members of two sets of numbers was basic to the work on cardinal numbers, just as the relationship of order between the members of one set of numbers develops the idea of ordinal numbers. Many other examples will be apparent.

Earlier in the book, arrow diagrams were used to represent certain relations. Members of one set may be linked to members of another set by an arrow which represents the relation.

Four examples are shown in Fig. 81. In (A) children's names are linked to items of their clothing and (B) represents a similar type of relationship in number work, the numbers 3, 4 and 5 being linked to numbers which are 2 more in each case. These regulations are both one-to-one, since each member of the first set is related to only one member of the second set. The first set is known as the *domain* and the second set (to which members of the first set are linked) is called the *co-domain.*

In examples (C) and (D), the relation is many-to-one because more than one member of the domain is related to one member of the co-domain. In (D) it should be realized that $3^2 = 9$ and $(^-3)^2 = {}^-3 \times {}^-3 = 9$ also (see negative numbers in Chapter 5).

In the two types of relation (A) and (B) above, any member of the domain is related to only one member of the co-domain and such relations are called *functions* or *mappings.* Figure (B) above, for example, could be described as a one-to-one mapping and we would say that 3 was mapped on to 5, 4 is mapped on to 6, etc.

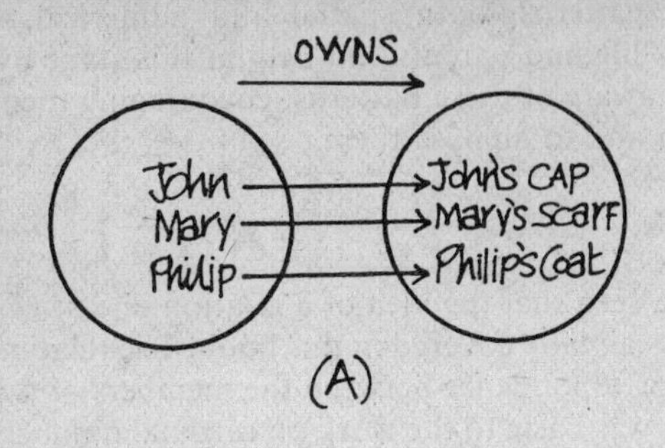

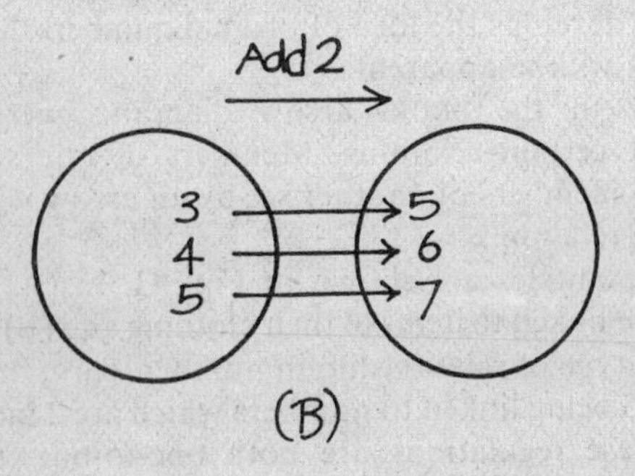

81. Relations.

Most of the graphs which children draw are graphs of functions. The domain is usually along the horizontal axis and the co-domain is on the vertical axis. Examination of the graphs drawn in the previous chapter will show that for any value along the horizontal axis, there is only one value corresponding on the vertical axis. For example, in the graph of Fig. 78, a numerator was related to its denominator and in the graph of Fig. 79, we have the relationship between the set of ages and the set of numbers.

Sometimes children draw diagrams to illustrate functions or mappings in a manner which differs somewhat from the

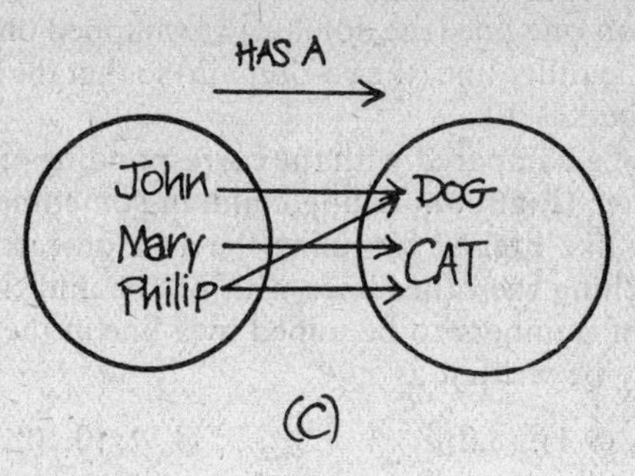

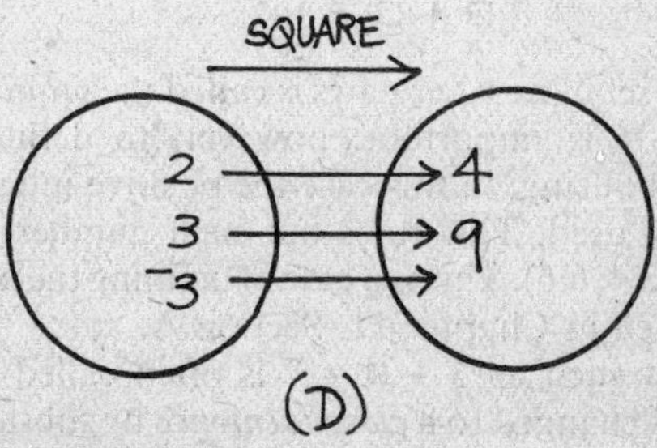

81. Relations.

---

normal type of graph. In each of the two diagrams below,

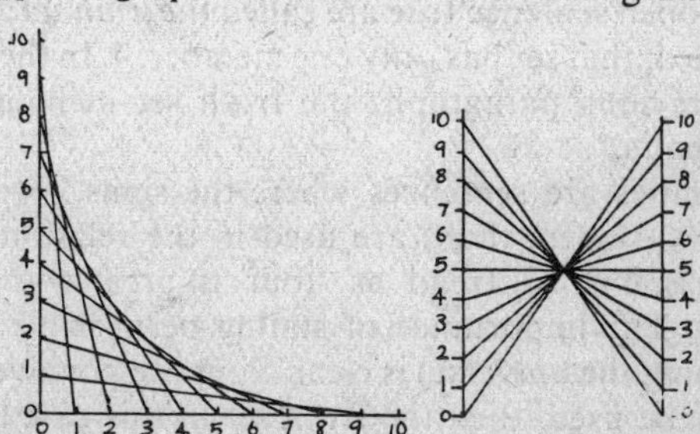

82. The numbers in one set (the domain) are mapped out on to the members of the other set (the co-domain) so that the sum of the two numbers is ten.

the numbers on one line (the domain) are mapped on to the numbers on the other line (the co-domain) so that the sum of the two numbers is 10.
These should be compared with the corresponding graph in the last chapter (Fig. 76). Young children sometimes construct graphs like Fig. 82 by ruling the axes on cardboard and then stitching the other lines with needle and thread.

The pairs of numbers to be joined by a line in the above diagrams may be written as

$$(10,0), (9,1), (8,2), \ldots \quad \ldots (1,9), (0,10)$$

each pair being a solution of the relation

$$\square + \square = 10$$

and the whole set of number pairs is called the *solution set* of this relation. It is important, however, to define which numbers we are using; in this case the positive integers and zero are being used. This rules out such number pairs as $(8\frac{1}{2}, 1\frac{1}{2})$ and $(3{\cdot}4, 6{\cdot}6)$. This is a case of defining the universal set, as explained in Chapter 11, Section A.

A statement such as $3 + \square = 7$ is often called an *open sentence* and is changed to a *closed sentence* by substituting a number from a solution set. If 4 is substituted, the statement is correct and the closed sentence is true; substitution of 5 would make it false, of course. The value, or values, which make an open sentence true are called the *truth set* and in the case quoted, that set has only one member, 4. In the example of the previous paragraph, the truth set includes all the number pairs.

Inequalities are sentences where the signs $>$ (is greater than) or $<$ (is less than) are used in the relationship. An example is $4 > \square$ (read as 'four is greater than some number'). The importance of stating permissible numbers (i.e. defining the universe) is clear. Suppose positive integers only may be used, then the truth set in this case is 3, 2, 1. Another example is $8 + \square < 16$, again using positive integers only. The truth set here is 7, 6, 5, 4, 3, 2, 1. If positive numbers (i.e. not integers only) were allowed, values such as 7·4, 4·15, etc. would have been possible and there would be an infinite number of members of the truth set, which would range from just under 8 (but not including 8), to just over zero.

A further example is $5 > \square > 2$, which can be read as 'the required number lies between 5 and 2' (i.e. is less than 5 and greater than 2). If integers only are allowed, the solution set has two members, 4 and 3, but if all numbers are allowed, there would be an infinite number of members of the solution set, lying between 5 and 2, but not including 5 and 2.

Generalisation

In the example of Fig. 82, which shows numbers whose sum is 10, the relationship was given and the task was to illustrate it. The reverse problem is where the illustration or some practical problem is given, and the pattern or relationship has to be found. For instance, examples were given earlier of sequences of numbers where the next terms had to be found. This type of problem is basic to a great deal of mathematics and can be a starting point for work in algebra.

In the chapter on shape, a formula was developed to obtain the sum of the angles of any plane figure with n sides. If the results had been tabulated for figures with 3, 4, 5, 6, . . . sides, a pattern could have been detected in the results:

Number of sides	*Sum of angles in right-angles*	*Sum of angles in straight-angles*
3	2	1
4	4	2
5	6	3
6	8	4

Possibly no immediate relationship between the figures in the first two columns is seen, but the figures in the last column are clearly always two less than those in the first column. So if n is the number of sides of the figure, the sum of the angles is $n - 2$ straight-angles, which is $2n - 4$ right-angles.

Sometimes it is easy to state the next term in a sequence, but difficult to find some expression which will enable us to find any term, this is usually called 'finding the general term'. As a simple illustration, at the start of this chapter we considered a young child with a series of coloured rods – yellow, red, yellow, red, etc. – and a child of this age would normally say that the next rod was yellow. He would then be able to say that the following rod would be red. But his only way of saying what colour was the 99th rod would be to find the colours of the preceding 98. An older child, however, would reason that the odd numbered rods were yellow and the even ones red, so the 99th would be yellow since 99 is an odd number. This step requires mathematical thought; there has been the vital step from concrete experiences, to an abstract deduction. This is what we have to encourage the child to do.

Another example comes from a spatial pattern. There is a series of numbers known as triangular numbers, since counters representing each may be arranged in triangular patterns:

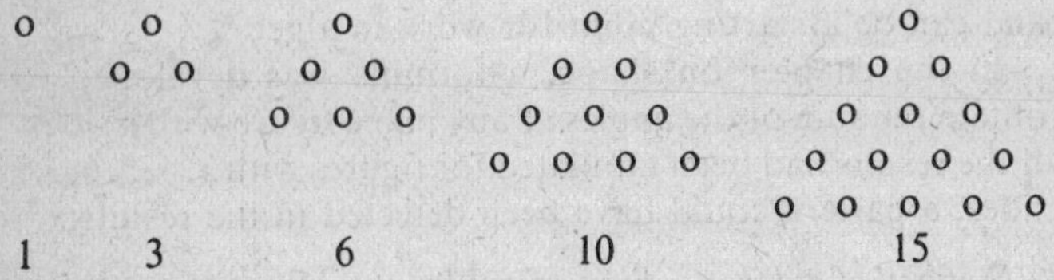

```
o    o       o          o           o
    o o     o o        o o         o o
           o o o      o o o       o o o
                     o o o o     o o o o
                                o o o o o
1    3       6          10          15
```

A child being shown these patterns may be able to say what the next number is. It is interesting to ask how this conclusion has been reached. Some will have taken the numbers themselves, 1, 3, 6, 10, 15, and noticed that they increase by 2, 3, 4 and 5 respectively. Others will look at the patterns and notice the number of extra counters each time. Some may find other ways.

The next step is to find a means of predicting any particular triangular number, e.g. the 20th. Again this may be approached in various ways. One method is to look at the diagram and see that

$$\begin{aligned}\text{the 5th number} &= 5 + \text{4th number}\\ &= 5 + 4 + \text{3rd number}\\ &= 5 + 4 + 3 + \text{2nd number}\\ &= 5 + 4 + 3 + 2 + \text{1st number}\\ &= 5 + 4 + 3 + 2 + 1.\end{aligned}$$

So the twentieth number could be found in a similar manner by adding all the numbers from 1 to 20 inclusive.

Although a method of solving the problem has now been found, it is not very suitable for large numbers; try finding the 100th triangular number, for example. Can we, therefore, find an easy way of adding the numbers from 1 to 20 inclusive? Arrange the numbers like this:

$$\begin{array}{cc} 20 & 1 \\ 19 & 2 \\ 18 & 3 \\ \cdots & \cdots \\ 11 & 10 \end{array}$$

Each row adds up to 21 and there will be 10 rows, so the answer is 210. This shows an easy method of adding the first 20 numbers and can be expressed in a formula to find the first n numbers. For n numbers the sum of each row would be $n + 1$ and there would be $n/2$ rows, giving a total of $n/2 \times (n + 1)$. This, therefore, is also the general term for a triangular number and it may be used to find any number in the series, e.g. the 30th number will be $30/2 \times (30 + 1)$, i.e. 465.

This problem is given as an example. It may not be met by pupils in some schools, but illustrates the way that generalisation from a practical example to a formula can be an introduction to the ideas of algebra. The derivation of some formula or expression from a problem or the substitution of values into a formula give an understanding of the idea of using letters to represent numbers.

RATIO AND PROPORTION

The idea of proportionality is a fundamental one, not only within mathematics. We talk about a building being well-proportioned and say that a proportion of the proceeds of some money-raising effort is to be given to charity. Proportion is basic to a great deal of mathematics and much of the work already covered in this book has made use of the principle. Spatial work with similar figures, multiplication tables, equivalent fractions – these are a few of the topics which make use of and develop the child's idea of proportion.

On page 117, the idea of scale was introduced with respect to making plans or maps. Consider two similar figures, the lengths on one being three times the corresponding lengths on the other, i.e. a scale factor of 3. One way of making such an enlargement is to take a point outside the original figure and to draw lines from it through the vertices of the figures as a series of rays from the point. The second figure, known as the *image* from the enlargement, is obtained by drawing lines parallel to the sides of the original figure to intersect the rays. The method is shown in the diagram.

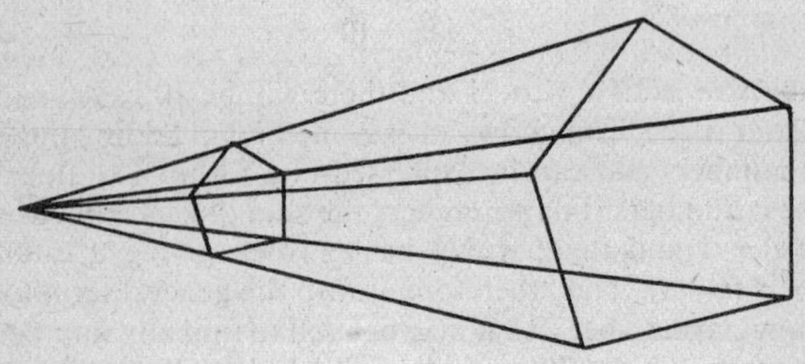

83. Enlargement.

A similar method may be used for reducing the size of a figure. In the example above, the length of any side of the image is three times the length of the corresponding side on the original figure. And the same is true for any corresponding lengths on the figures, e.g. heights. The *ratio* of the lengths on the image to corresponding lengths on the original is 'three to one'; this may be written 3:1 or $\frac{3}{1}$.

The next diagram shows two similar triangles (ABC and ADE) which could be drawn on squared paper or constructed with rubber bands on a nail-board, and in this case it will be seen from the two sides AB and AD that the ratio of one to the other is 3:5.

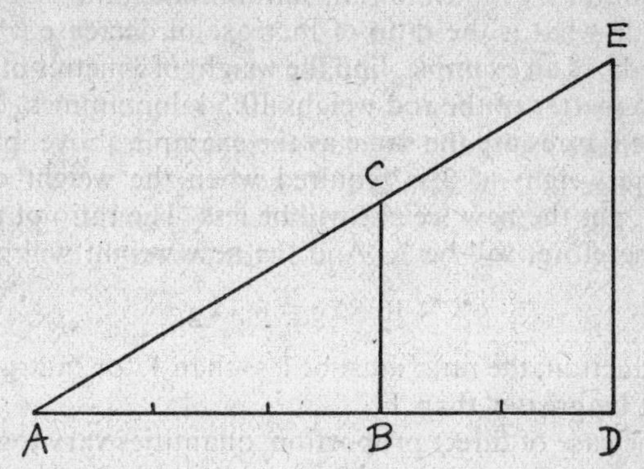

84. Similar triangles where the AB is $\frac{3}{5}$ the length of AD.

Suppose the length of DE is known, say x cm, then the length of BC will be $\frac{3}{5}$ of x. The advantage of using the fractional form, rather than the form 3:5, becomes apparent. Also notice that ratios which are equivalent fractions are themselves equivalent. For example the ratio $\frac{3}{5}$ is equivalent to the ratio $\frac{6}{10}$.

There are examples of the use of ratio in many other calculations. A recipe may give lists of ingredients sufficient to make a meal for 6 people but you wish to make it for 4 people. Then the quantity of each ingredient must be reduced in the ratio of $\frac{4}{6}$ or $\frac{2}{3}$. 300 grammes of fat, for example, would become $\frac{2}{3} \times 300$ grammes, i.e. 200 grammes.

There are cases where the different measures are altered in the same ratio. For example, if 3 metres of dress material costs £10.50, the cost of 5 metres will be in the ratio of $\frac{5}{3}$ of the original cost, i.e.

$$\frac{5}{3} \times £10.50 = £17.50.$$

This type of calculation is known as *direct proportion*. If we represent it graphically, it is a straight line graph passing through the origin; see Fig. 74 in the last chapter.

Whenever a problem of this nature is met, the first step is to decide what is the ratio of increase or decrease which is required. As an example, find the weight of 3 metres of metal rod if 5 metres of the rod weighs 10.5 kilogrammes. Notice that the figures are the same as the example above, but this time the weight of 3 is required when the weight of 5 is known, i.e. the new weight will be less. The ratio of reduction, therefore, will be $\frac{3}{5}$. And the new weight will be

$$\frac{3}{5} \times 10{\cdot}5\ \text{kg} = 6{\cdot}3\ \text{kg}.$$

For reduction, the ratio must be less than 1, for enlargement it must be greater than 1.

In the case of direct proportion, quantities vary together. Thus the price of the dress material increased as the length increased and the weight of the metal decreased as the length decreased. However, there is a type of proportion where the quantities vary inversely, i.e. one increases as the other decreases and vice versa. This is known as *inverse proportion.* As an example, suppose a car journey takes 45 minutes when the overall speed is 40 km per hour, how long will the journey take if the speed is increased to 60 km per hour? The method is similar to that of direct proportion, but notice in this case that the speed has been increased, so the time taken will be decreased. The ratio of this decrease will obviously be $\frac{40}{60}$ which is equivalent to $\frac{2}{3}$. Hence the time taken at the new speed will be:

$$\frac{2}{3} \times 45\ \text{minutes} = 30\ \text{minutes}.$$

The graph of the direct proportion relationship is a straight line through the origin, but the graph of an inverse proportion relationship is a curve known as a rectangular hyperbola. This has been shown in Fig. 77 in the last chapter. Reference was made there to rectangles of constant area. Suppose we draw a series of rectangles, each of area 24 square. An obvious one is that with length 12 cm and breadth 2 cm. If the length is decreased from 12 cm, the breadth will be increased; clearly inverse proportion. Also if we denote the length by l and the breadth by b, then $l \times b = 24$. This gives the equation of the curve when we draw the graph, by taking a series of appropriate values for l and b, plotting the points and joining them.

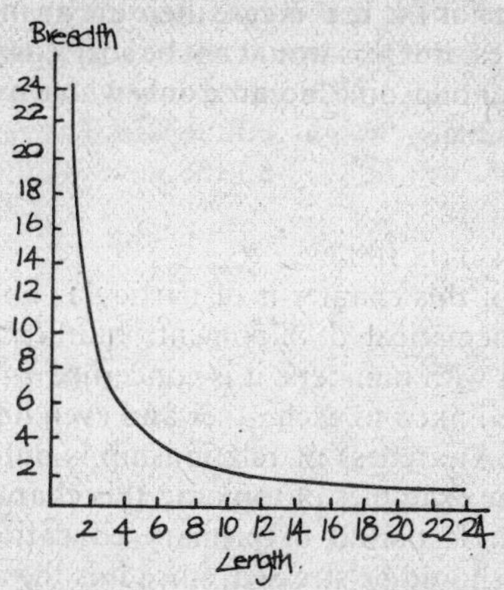

85. Graph of the equation $l \times b = 24$.

With axes for x and y the equation of a rectangular hyperbola is $xy = k$, where k is a constant which depends on the particular problem.

A word of warning is necessary, however, in the case of inverse proportion since calculated results may be unrealistic. There is no difficulty in the case of the rectangles of constant area, since all values obtained from the graph represent possible rectangles. But with the earlier problem about car speeds, some impossible results can be obtained. For example, a journey of 3 minutes may be obtained by travelling at a speed of 600 km per hour! It might be questioned even whether the earlier answer of 30 minutes may be little more than a rough indication since much depends on traffic conditions. This stresses once more the importance of thinking about answers to problems and whether they seem reasonable.

Care has to be exercised particularly when graphs or statistics are used to make predictions. When dealing with numbers only, all solutions are possible. For example, the rectangular hyperbola $x y = 24$ may represent two numbers whose product is 24. In this case there are an infinite number of possibilities. But this would not be so if x or y represented, say, a number of people, because only whole numbers would then be possible.

SUGGESTIONS FOR HELP

The theme of this chapter is of particular importance to a child's mathematical development. Mathematics is more than dealing with numbers; it is concerned with how things relate or are linked to each other and even how those links are related. Awareness of relationship is built up over the years and the examples of topics in this chapter can extend over the whole period of primary education. The word 'awareness' should be stressed, since it is the ability to look for and discover relationship that has to be developed. It cannot be taught in the way that a set of rules may be. Some relationships may occur frequently and can help in the solution of problems; others may be quite unique and require thought before a solution can be found.

The examples given in this chapter are not so important for the content of the examples as for the ideas and methods that they typify as relationships are sought and made use of. Encourage children to look for relationships. With very young children, provide opportunities for comparisons, e.g. 'is greater than'. With older children, looking at maps or plans, discussing scale models and similar activities can form a starting point. Numerical examples can take the form of games, such as guessing the relation between numbers: the child gives a number, say 3, and the parent replies 5; the child says 6, the parent 8; the child guesses that two is being added each time. Examples can be more complicated, e.g. 2 and 5, 4 and 9, 6 and 13, etc., where the original number is being multiplied by 2 and 1 added. An explanation such as the last is sometimes difficult and it is better to express it as a general term, e.g. n and $2n + 1$.

Generalisation, such as this, may arise from practical activities, e.g. folding a sheet of paper:

No. of folds	0	1	2	3	4	5	6
No. of thicknesses of paper	1	2	4	8	16	32	64

In this case, if n is the number of folds, the relationship is 2^n.

It will have become clear from this chapter that one of the best ways of showing relationships is by the use of a graph, and children having difficulties with problems may achieve a better understanding if they can be represented in graphical form.

11
SOME NEW TOPICS EXPLAINED

In this chapter it is proposed to explain in more detail some of the topics which have been introduced earlier. Some parents may wish to know more of these topics so that they may better understand them. Included also are some additional topics which may be found in the work of some primary schools.

A. SETS

In the primary schools the main work with sets is concerned with the way in which sets are made up, put together, partitioned and so on, and is related to the development of the child's understanding, particularly through classification. The work is done very largely with concrete materials (plastic counters, toys, etc.) or by drawing. Work on sets in the secondary school develops an algebra where the various parts and processes are expressed in symbols. Some of this symbolism will be given here, but the work may also be explained by the use of diagrams known as Venn diagrams. It will be seen that the work in the primary school makes use of simple Venn diagrams.

The idea of a set has been explained already: a collection of different things. Often it is necessary to define the area under consideration; this is called the *universe of discourse*, or more briefly, the universe, and is denoted by U. Thus if our set is the set of 8-year-old girls, are we talking about all such girls, or the girls in a particular school, or the girls in a room, etc.? If we are talking about children at Cedar Avenue School, then this is our universe (shown below as a rectangle) and the set of 8-year-old girls lies in that universe. The Venn diagram is as follows:

86. Venn diagram.

The individual girls of the set are called the *elements* or the members of that set. It is possible to have sets within the set of girls; for example there may be the set of girls with fair hair and the set of girls with dark hair. These form sub-sets of the larger set. It may be decided to have a third sub-set consisting of girls with ginger hair, but then it is discovered that there are no such girls in the 8-year-olds at that school. This means that this set has no members and it is called an *empty set.*

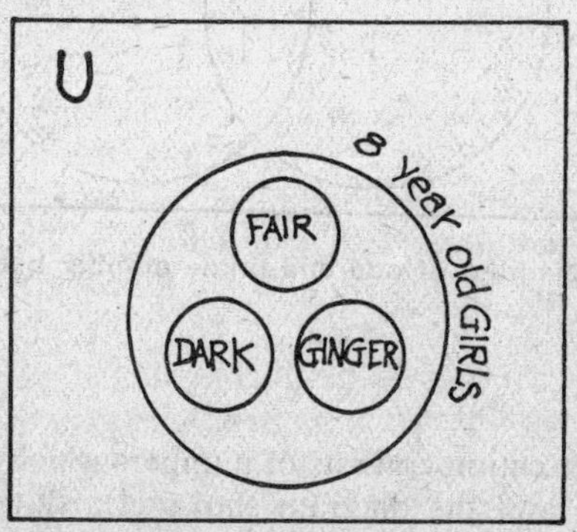

87. Venn diagram of girls by hair colour.

Most of the common terms of manipulation of sets were explained in Chapter 4. If two or more sets are combined, we speak of their *union*, if a set is split into sub-sets we call it *partition* of the set. And if two or more sets can have common members it is called their *intersection.*

There are symbols to denote these processes. Firstly a set is usually written within brackets known as braces, e.g. A ={8-year-old girls} means that A is the set of 8-year-old girls. There are two ways of defining a set: either by stating some property to identify the members, or by listing the members. For example, we could describe a set N as:

N={odd numbers between 10 and 20}
or N={11, 13, 15, 17, 19}

If we illustrate this with a Venn diagram which also shows P = {prime numbers between 10 and 20}, the diagram is:

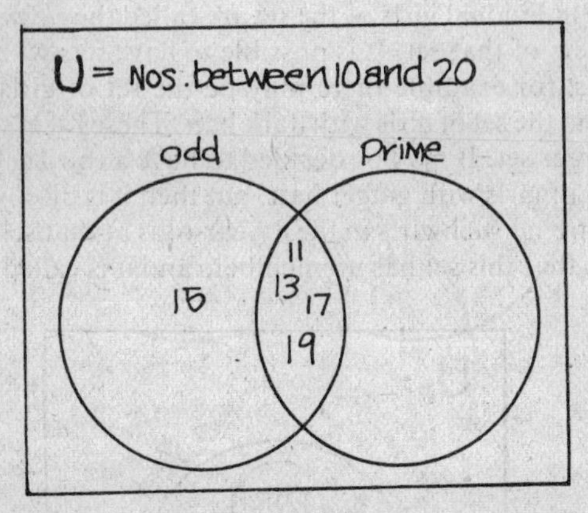

88. Venn diagram of odd and prime number between ten and twenty.

The intersection consists of numbers which are both odd and prime and the diagram shows clearly that the set of prime numbers which are not odd is an empty set in this case.

The two sets D and E are seen to be sub-sets of the original set N. This is what one would expect, since the only even prime number is 2 and this is not in our universe.

The union of sets is denoted by the symbol $\cup$ and the intersection by $\cap$, so we could write:

$$N \cap P = \{11, 13, 17, 19\} = \text{set D, say.}$$
$$N \cup P = \{11, 13, 15, 17, 19\} = \text{set E, say.}$$

The two sets D and E are sub-sets of the original set N. This means that they are contained in N, although in the case of E the members are the same as the members of N.

It is not always necessary to define the universe if it is clear what that particular universe is. The following diagram shows the sets of multiples of 2, 3 and 5 from 10 to 30 inclusive.

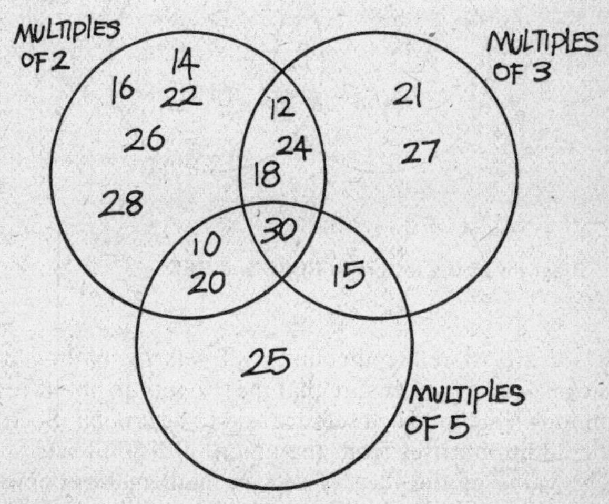

89. Diagram of multiples of two, three and five from ten to thirty inclusive.

If we had defined the universe as U = {numbers from 10 to 30 inclusive}, we would have to surround the above figure by a rectangle representing U and outside the circles would be the prime numbers. Notice the numbers which lie in the intersections of the sets and particularly 30, which is in the intersection of the three sets.

Suppose X = {letters of the word RED}
Y = {letters of the word BLUE}

There are 3 letters in the word RED and 4 in BLUE, so normal addition says that there are 7 letters in the two words. However, the union of the two sets, i.e. $X \cup Y$ has only 6 letters in the set, because the letter E is a member of both sets.

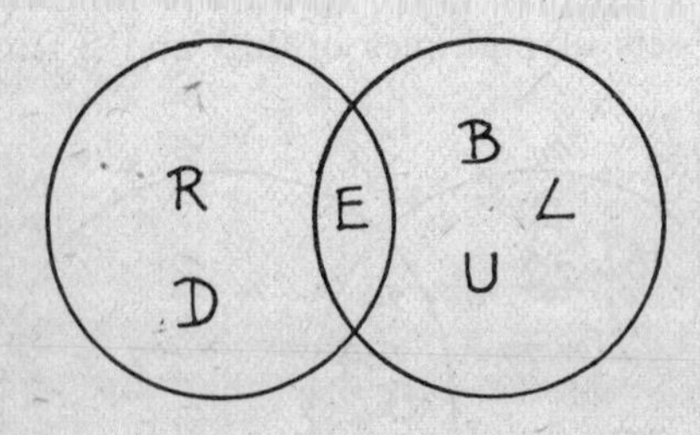

90. Diagram of the letters in BLUE and RED.

If we are to relate the union of sets to mathematical addition, we have to ensure that the two sets do not have any common elements. Such sets are said to be *disjoint*. So arithmetic addition arises from the union of disjoint sets.

The value of the idea of sets in mathematics comes in classification and in the structure of the subject. At a later stage in mathematics, the theory of sets has links with logic and with circuit design, both of which find an application in computer design.

An example of classification in mathematics comes from the different types of quadrilateral. These may be sorted in various ways, e.g. according to parallel and equal sides. But the work on symmetry of Chapter 8 provides a useful basis. Line and rotational symmetry are used as follows:

Quadrilateral with no symmetry (Q)

Trapezium (no symmetry) (T)

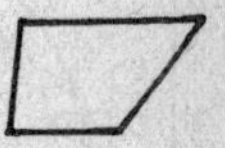

Kite (one axis) (K)

Parallelogram (rotational) (P)

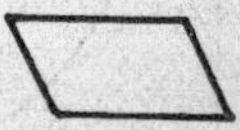

Rhombus (2 axes and rotational) (Rh)

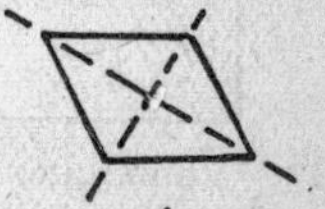

Rectangle (2 axes and rotational) (Re)

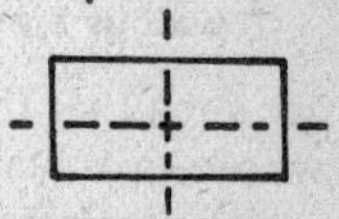

Square (4 axes and rotational) (S)

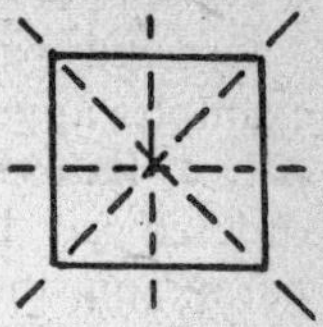

The Venn diagram is shown overleaf.

B. CARTESIAN PRODUCT

The idea of an ordered pair of numbers was introduced in Chapter 9. Basically it is two numbers written in a way in which the order matters, e.g. (3, 4). Often there is a series of ordered pairs, the first terms of which belong to one set of numbers and the second terms to another set of numbers. Thus the series of pairs:

(2,4), (3,9), (4,16), (5,25), (6,36)

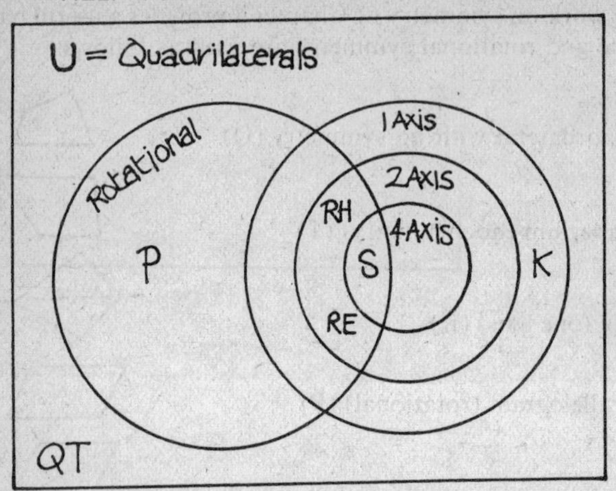

91. Venn diagram to show line and rotational symmetry of various types of quadrilateral.

are such that the second terms belong to the set of numbers whose members are the squares of the members of the first set of numbers.

Ordered pairs are used widely in mathematics. Two examples appear earlier in the book: the use of an ordered pair to fix a point on a plane and writing a fraction as an ordered pair. In the case of the number pairs listed in the last paragraph, there is a one-to-one relationship between the numbers in the first set and those in the second, since any number in the first set has to be paired with its square which appears in the second set. There are cases, however, where such a relation does not exist and any member of the first set may be paired with any member of the second set. To take an example, a girl may have 4 differently coloured blouses, denoted by set B = {red, blue, green, white}, and a set of 3 skirts denoted by S = {black, red, white}. She may select any blouse with any skirt to form an outfit. This can be shown on a diagram where each cross represents a possible outfit.

These results can be written as ordered pairs in the form (blouse colour, skirt colour). It is clear that there are 12 pos-

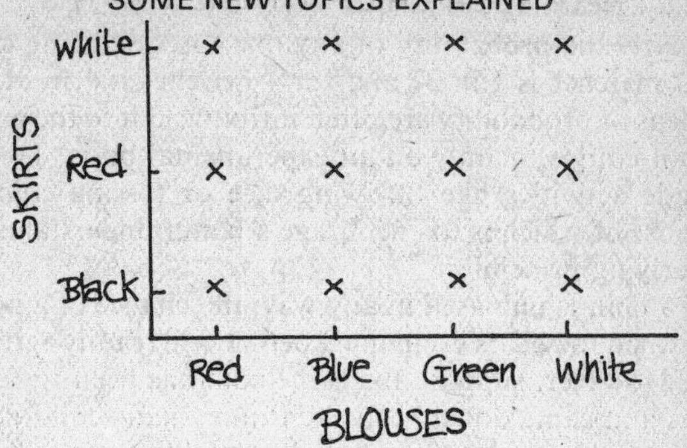

92. All the possible different colour combinations of skirts and blouses.

sible pairs and this is called the *cartesian product* or cross product of the two sets. It is written as $B \times S$ and is obtained by multiplying the number of members of the first set by the number of members of the second set, in this case 4×3. The result is important, since sometimes we do not wish to know the individual pairs, but only the total number of possible pairs. This is the case when we are dealing with probability. If we wished to find the possible results of two football matches we could write these as a series of number pairs of the type (1st result, 2nd result). The first result would be a member of the set $R_1 = \{$home win, away win, draw$\}$ and the second result a member of the set $R_2=\{$home win, away win, draw$\}$. Since there are three members of each set $R_1 \times R_2 = 9$, which represents the total possible results of the two matches.

This calculation could be extended to find the possible results of 3 matches which would give 27 possibilities, of 4 matches giving 81 possibilities, and so on.

C. PROBABILITY

The last section provides a useful introduction to the topic of probability. There are 9 possible outcomes of the results of 2 football matches and since there is only one final result, the probability of any one forecast being correct is 1 in 9.

Similarly the probability of any one forecast being correct for 3 matches is 1 in 27 and for 4 matches is 1 in 81.

Ideas of probability are often introduced into the primary school course, mainly on an experimental basis. This may include activities like throwing dice or tossing coins, the purpose of which is to encourage a better understanding of underlying principles.

If a coin is unbiased in any way, the chance of a head or tail, when tossed, is even; most people will readily agree with this. However, suppose the same coin has been tossed five times and came down head each time, many children (and many adults, too) will no longer say that there is an even chance for the sixth toss. Some will argue, in spite of the assurance that the coin is unbiased, that it now seems more likely to come down head than tail. Others will argue that, since the coin is unbiased, there has to be roughly the same number of heads as tails resulting from a series of tosses and since there have been heads in the first 5 tosses, the likelihood of tails in the next toss is increased. Both views are wrong, of course.

If the result of any event depends purely on chance, then the outcome is not affected in any way by earlier events. In the case of the sixth toss in the example above, there is still an equal chance of a head or a tail.

In mathematics, the probability of an event happening is defined as

$$\frac{\text{Number of ways that event can take place}}{\text{Total possible ways that event can and cannot take place}}$$

For the tossing of a coin, head can occur once and the total possibilities are 2 (head or tail), so the probability of a head for any toss is $\frac{1}{2}$.

Practical work in the primary school may involve tossing coins, the results for the whole class giving the outcome of a large number of tosses. Next, two coins may be tossed at the same time and the results recorded under the headings of '2 heads', '2 tails', and 'head/tail'. There is a difference here since head/tail is more likely to occur than the others because it includes two outcomes, HT and TH. The probability of 2 heads in this case is $\frac{1}{4}$, the probability of 2 tails is $\frac{1}{4}$ and the probability of 1 head and 1 tail is $\frac{1}{2}$. The experiment might be repeated with 3 or more coins and conclusions drawn. Notice, however, that the results above are theoretical results, which may differ from the practical results.

Throwing dice also provides interesting results. If one die is thrown, the probability of any one number being scored is $\frac{1}{6}$ and large numbers of throws are undertaken by pupils to see how far they agree with this theoretical result. If two dice are thrown and the scores added, we get a more complex result. Children will perform the experiment and record the scores but a theoretical table of frequencies may be compiled as follows:

Totals	*2*	*3*	*4*	*5*	*6*	*7*	*8*	*9*	*10*	*11*	*12*
	1,1	1,2	1,3	1,4	1,5	1,6					
		2,1	2,2	2,3	2,4	2,5	2,6				
			3,1	3,2	3,3	3,4	3,5	3,6			
Outcomes				4,1	4,2	4,3	4,4	4,5	4,6		
					5,1	5,2	5,3	5,4	5,5	5,6	
						6,1	6,2	6,3	6,4	6,5	6,6
Frequencies	*1*	*2*	*3*	*4*	*5*	*6*	*5*	*4*	*3*	*2*	*1*

From the table it is possible to calculate the theoretical probability of any score. The total frequencies is 36 and a score of 3 can occur in 2 ways, so the probability of a score of 3 is $\frac{2}{36}$ and similarly of scoring 8 is $\frac{5}{36}$. Notice that the total of the frequencies (i.e. 36) agrees with what is obtained by finding the cartesian product for two dice with 6 faces each, i.e. 6×6.

It does not follow, of course, that the experimental result will coincide with the predictions of the table. In other words, if 36 throws of two dice are made, we may expect 2 of the throws to give a total of 3 and 5 throws to give a total of 8, but the actual results could be very different. Experimental results would be discussed in class and various conclusions drawn.

D. CONSIDERATIONS OF ZERO

Zero, or nought, occupies a special place in our number system and children sometimes experience difficulty in consequence. It is not a counting (or natural) number since when we count we start with 1. Nevertheless it is an origin point when we are measuring with a ruler or tape and when we are using it as a number line. In these cases we are considering the ordinal aspect of number.

The concept is no easier when we are considering cardinal numbers, since nothing is not a recognizable quantity. It is possible to demonstrate 2 by showing 2 pencils, 2 books or 2 coins, but it is difficult to 'show' 0 of anything! One definition which is sometimes used in this respect is that 0 is the number of members of the empty set. Another aspect is when a number is subtracted from itself, e.g. 3 — 3 = 0.

But zero may also be defined as a limit in the same way that we define infinity, although this approach is not satisfactory for young children. Greater and greater numbers may be taken, forever increasing until ultimately (i.e. in the limit) infinity is reached. In the same way, numbers may be decreased indefinitely until, in the limit, zero is reached.

When there is a number such as 200 or 0·05, the 0's are regarded as *place holders*, their purpose being to indicate the value assigned to the other figures (in this case 2 and 5). We do not 'read' the 0's in a number such as 200 in the way that we read 5 and 4 in 254.

However, it is when we are doing operations involving 0 that we have difficulty in finding real everyday practical situations. When, for example, do we add 0 to anything in real life? Addition or subtraction of 0 to other numbers does not alter the value of those numbers and this unique property leads us to call 0 the *identity element* for addition and subtraction.

Multiplication and division involving zero is equally difficult to instance in everyday life. Children may accept the idea of 3 people having no money, so together they have nothing, or $3 \times 0 = 0$, but the imagination has to be stretched to think of someone dividing nothing between three people, so that each received nothing, i.e. $0 \div 3 = 0$.

Division of 3 by 0 is even more difficult. It can be found by successive division by increasingly small quantities until a limit is reached.

$\frac{3}{1/10}$ means 3 divided by $1/10$, or how many tenths in 3?

The answer is 30. So we have, by working in a similar fashion:

$$3/1 = 3$$
$$\frac{3}{1/10} = 30$$
$$\frac{3}{1/100} = 300$$
$$\frac{3}{1/1000000} = 3000000$$

As the value of the denominator becomes smaller, the value of the whole fraction becomes greater and eventually we find that $3/0$ becomes infinitely great.

E. THE NUMBER LAWS

In the last section 0 was said to be the identity element for addition and subtraction because adding or subtracting 0 left a number unchanged. In a similar manner, 1 is the identity element for multiplication and division, because, for any number, n, multiplying or dividing by 1 leaves the number unchanged, i.e. $n \times 1 = n$ and $n \div 1 = n$.

Apart from the special properties that arise from the identity elements, they are important since they give meaning to the idea of an inverse. Inverses were explained in

Chapter 5, addition and subtraction were said to be inverse processes, as were multiplication and division. We now take the idea a step further.

We say that $^{-}2$ is the *additive inverse* of 2 because their sum is 0. This means that instead of subtracting, we could add the inverse element, i.e. $5 + {}^{-}2$ is equivalent to $5 - 2$. One obvious outcome of this is that we could dispense with the idea of subtraction.

In a similar manner, the *multiplicative inverse* of 4 is $\frac{1}{4}$, because their product is 1. Sometimes the multiplicative inverse is called the reciprocal, e.g. the reciprocal of $\frac{3}{4}$ is $\frac{4}{3}$. Since division is the inverse of multiplication, instead of dividing by a number we could multiply by its multiplicative inverse. Thus $8 \div 4$ is equivalent to $8 \times \frac{1}{4}$, since both equal 2. This example gives meaning to the rule for dividing by a fraction, usually put into the words 'turn it upside down and multiply'. Since the multiplicative inverse of $\frac{2}{3}$ is $\frac{3}{2}$, the example $8 \div \frac{2}{3}$ is equivalent to $8 \times \frac{3}{2}$, which equals 12. As a further example, $\frac{2}{5} \div \frac{3}{4} = \frac{2}{5} \times \frac{4}{3} = \frac{8}{15}$. However, it was pointed out earlier that division by fractions probably will not be covered in the primary school except in simple cases of a practical nature, such as 'how many $\frac{1}{3}$rds are there in 2?'

The identity elements are part of the fundamental laws of arithmetic, laws which most of us use without really being aware of them. That is until we do some calculation which violates these laws and results in a wrong answer. Some of these laws have been mentioned earlier. The *commutative law* for addition and for multiplication is one of the simplest of the laws and states that the order of operation does not matter. In symbolic form, if a and b are two numbers, then $a + b = b + a$ and $a \times b = b \times a$. This law was stated in the section on multiplication in Chapter 5, where the symmetry of the multiplication table was linked to the law. The commutative law does not apply to subtraction and division.

If a, b and c are numbers, then the *associative laws* for addition and multiplication are:

$$a + (b + c) = (a + b) + c$$
$$a \times (b \times c) = (a \times b) \times c$$

The laws are really stating that if we are adding or multiplying three numbers, it does not matter which two we operate on first. As fairly simple examples, the laws can be helpful in doing mental calculations. Adding numbers such as 18, 57, and 22, the fact that $18 + 22 = 40$, to which can then be added the 57, makes for quicker and less error-prone calculation than adding the numbers in the order written.

The *distributive laws* of multiplication over addition say that for three numbers a, b and c,

$$a \times (b + c) = a \times b + a \times c$$
$$(b + c) \times a = b \times a + c \times a$$

These laws are used repeatedly when multiplying numbers greater than 10; they, too, are used in the section on multiplication in Chapter 5. An example is as follows:

$$\begin{aligned} 8 \times 53 &= 8 \times (50 + 3) \\ &= 8 \times 50 + 8 \times 3 \text{ (\textit{Distributive law})} \\ &= 8 \times (5 \times 10) + 8 \times 3 \\ &= (8 \times 5) \times 10 + 8 \times 3 \text{ (\textit{Associative law})} \\ &= 40 \times 10 + 8 \times 3 \\ &= 400 + 24 \\ &= 424 \end{aligned}$$

The same principles are employed in the normal vertical setting down of multiplication:

$$\begin{array}{rrl} & 34 & \\ \times & 26 & \\ \hline & 204 & \text{(i.e. } 34 \times 6\text{)} \\ & 680 & \text{(i.e. } 34 \times 20\text{)} \\ \hline & 884 & \end{array}$$

It is these laws which enable us to multiply numbers of any size with knowledge of no more than the multiplication tables up to 10.

F. NUMBER BASES AND PLACE VALUE

In the section 'Hundreds, tens and units' of Chapter 5, the idea of using number systems other than our normal system to base 10 was explained, particularly with reference to Dienes' M.A.B. apparatus. Some readers may be interested to take this matter further, although – as explained earlier – not all schools do such work.

In our normal system of numbers, we count in tens; we call this the base. If we add 1 and 9 we do not have a digit for ten, but write 10, knowing that the 1 in this case represents 1 ten. Similarly when we add 1 to 99, we obtain 100 where the 1 now represents a hundred, i.e. ten 10s, or 10^2. When we reach 1000, the 1 represents 10^3, for 10000 the 1 represents 10^4 and so on. When a child writes a number in columns, each column represents 10 times the column to the immediate right, like this:

10^4	10^3	10^2	10^1	1
5	7	3	2	8

The same is true for all number bases and may be generalized by using the letter b to denote the base. The columns are then as follows:

b^4	b^3	b^2	b^1	1
1	1	1	1	1

Each digit of the number 11111 represents b times the 1 immediately on the right of it.

If we were using base 4, then b = 4 and the display is

256	64	16	4	1
1	1	1	1	1

The figure on the right means 1 unit, the next figure to the left means 1 four, the next means 1 sixteen and so on, so that in our normal base 10 system, the number above represents

$$256 + 64 + 16 + 4 + 1 \text{ or } 341.$$

We could write

$$11111_{\text{base } 4} = 341_{\text{base } 10}$$

Similarly $231_{base\,4}$ represents $2 \times 16 + 3 \times 4 + 1 = 45_{base\,10}$

Whatever number bases we use, there is a limit to the number of digits possible in that base. Looking at the columns of the base 4 number above, it will be realized that if we had 3 in the units column and then added 1, we should have 4, but 4 is represented by a 1 in the second column. Hence the digits which are used in base 4 are 0, 1, 2, 3 only. The same applies in any base: the number of digits we require, including 0, is equal to the number base. Thus for base 6 we require the six digits 0, 1, 2, 3, 4, 5, for base 8 we require the eight digits 0, 1, 2, 3, 4, 5, 6, 7 and for base 2 we need only 0 and 1.

It is a useful exercise to start with 1 in any base and add on 1 successively. This is done below for bases 10, 3 and 2.

Base 10	*Base 3*	*Base 2*
Tens units	9 3 units	8 4 2 units
1	1	1
+ 1	+ 1	+ 1
2	2	1 0
+ 1	+ 1	+ 1
3	1 0	1 1
+ 1	+ 1	+ 1
4	1 1	1 0 0
1	1	1
5	1 2	1 0 1
1	1	1
6	2 0	1 1 0
1	1	1
7	2 1	1 1 1
1	1	1
8	2 2	1 0 0 0
1	1	1
9	1 0 0	1 0 0 1
1	1	1
1 0	1 0 1	1 0 1 0

It is possible to perform calculations involving any of the four rules in any base, although primary school children would probably perform addition and subtration only. Such calculations should be worked in terms of the base that is being used and not by translating numbers into the decimal system. In particular, when there is any 'carry over' from one column to the next it is essential to remember the base being used. The following addition is in base 6, and sub-totals are shown:

```
   2 5 3
 + 1 4 4
 -------
     1 1    adding units
   1 3 0    adding 6s
   3 0 0    adding 36s
 -------
   4 4 1
 -------
```

The intermediate lines are not essential but are inserted to make clear the processes. Notice that the answer is read 'four four one' and *not* 'four hundred and forty-one' because these are not hundreds and tens.

This subtraction is in base 4:

```
   3 3 0
 - 1 2 1
 -------
   2 0 3
```

It is impossible to take 1 from 0 in the units column, so a 4 (N.B. not a ten!) is added to the 0; then $4 - 1 = 3$.

Either reduce the 3 to 2, then subtract 2; $2 - 2 = 0$

Or add 1 to the 2 of 121 to make it 3; then $3 - 3 = 0$.

Finally, the 16s column is worked, $3 - 1 = 2$.

Much more work can be done on number bases, but the main purpose in introducing this to primary school children is to help them to understand the principle stated above, that the value of the placing of digits in a number is

$$b^3 \quad b^2 \quad b^1 \quad 1.$$

In particular, the digits in our decimal numbers indicate successive multiplication by 10 as we move to the left. We call this the understanding of place value. It was explained in earlier chapters that many errors that children make with calculations stem from a failure to appreciate place value. Examples are the omission of a 0 from an answer when doing multiplication or division so that an answer such as 207 is written as 27; and mistakes in subtraction involving 'carry over', particularly when this has to be done twice, e.g.

$$\begin{array}{r} 6\ 0\ 3 \\ -\underline{2\ 4\ 7} \\ 3\ 5\ 6 \end{array}$$

A useful type of apparatus to assist children with work on number bases is the Dienes' M.A.B. material which was described in Chapter 5. It is rather expensive for individual purchase, but is very effective when used correctly.

G. CLOCK ARITHMETIC

Clock arithmetic is introduced in some schools, mainly as a topic of interest, although it is developed in mathematics into modular arithmetic and then into an important branch of the subject, group theory. Care must be taken not to confuse this work with the work on number bases set out above, as there are links and similarities.

The usual approach is with an ordinary clock face carrying the numbers 1 to 12.

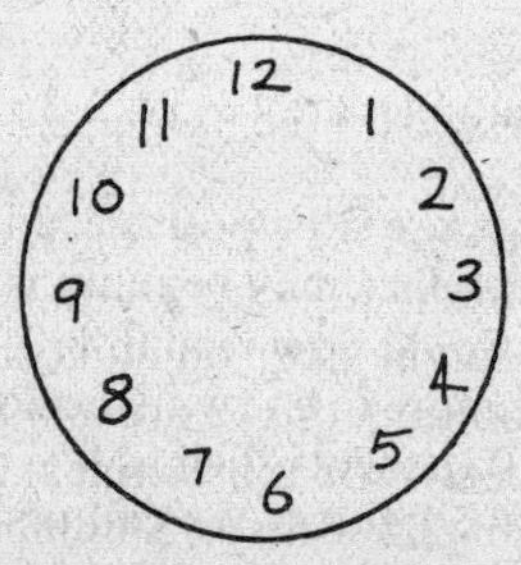

93. An ordinary clock face.

We add by going around the clock face, e.g. $3+5=8$. However, $8+6=2$, $4+9=1$, $9+7=4$, etc. These results are achieved by finding the first number, then counting the second number in a clockwise direction, as we do with time, i.e. 8 o'clock + 6 hours is 2 o'clock.

Subtraction may be performed in the same way, but this time by counting the second number 'backwards', i.e. anti-clockwise. Thus we have $3-6=9$ and $5-10=7$. Multiplication and division are also possible, as explained below.

There is no reason why this should be restricted to the familiar 1 to 12 of household clocks. Any number of digits may be used on the clock face. For example, we could use the numbers 1 to 5.

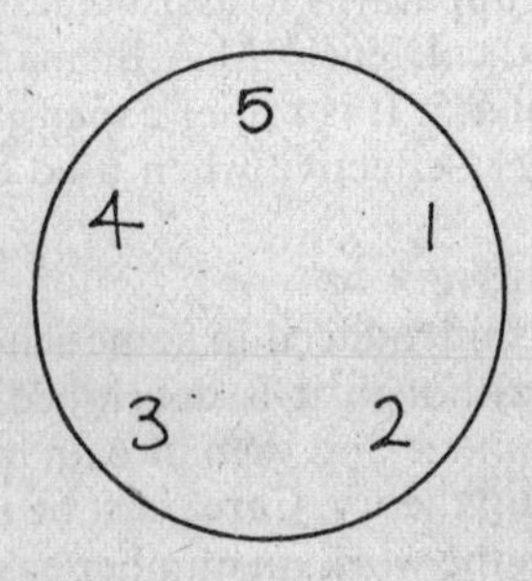

94. Clock numbered one to five.

In this case, some examples are $4+3=2$, $3+5=3$, $2-4=3$ and $1-4=2$.

Two developments are now possible. Firstly the highest number on each clock face may be replaced by 0; in the last diagram, the digits would now read 0, 1, 2, 3, 4. This brings the clock arithmetic more in line with the normal arithmetic, since we now have statements such as $0+4=4$, in the case of the clock with five figures. We call this new arithmetic modular arithmetic and denote each system by a modulo number. This latter is the number of figures on the clock face, so that, in the case of the last example, it would be modulo 5. Results are written in the form:

$$4 + 3 = 2 \text{ (modulo 5)}$$
$$3 + 0 = 3 \text{ (modulo 5)}$$
$$2 - 4 = 3 \text{ (modulo 5)}$$
$$1 - 4 = 2 \text{ (modulo 5)}$$

Writing 'modulo 5' gives meaning to statements which otherwise seem strange.

Secondly, it is possible to construct tables showing the result of addition and multiplication in modular arithmetic. Below is the clock face for modulo 8.

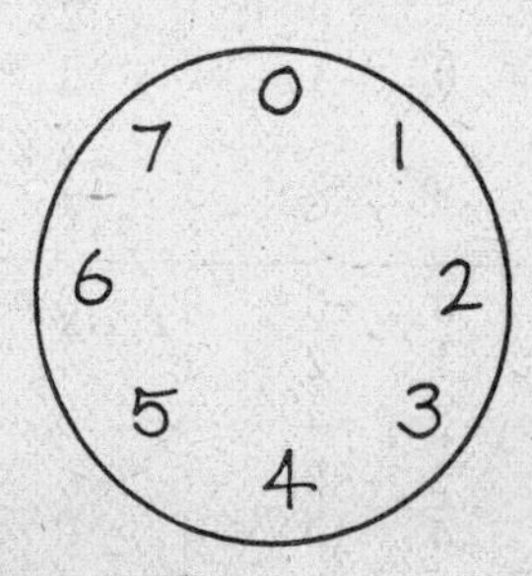

95. Clock numbered nought to seven (modulo eight).

The results of multiplication are obtained by repeated addition, thus $3 \times 7 = 7 + 7 + 7$, giving an answer of 5 (modulo 8). Similarly division may be done by repeated subtraction until 0 is reached, e.g. $4 \div 2$, we subtract 2 twice, and for $1 \div 3$, we start at 1 and subtract 3 three times before we reach 0, so that $1 \div 3 = 3$ (modulo 8).

To use the tables below, addition and multiplication results are obtained in the usual way by finding the intersection of appropriate row and column. To subtract, using the addition table, e.g. $1 - 4$, find 4 down the side, then find 1 in the corresponding row, then read to the top, giving an answer of 5.

The addition and multiplication tables for modulo 8 are as follows:

+	0	1	2	3	4	5	6	7
0	0	1	2	3	4	5	6	7
1	1	2	3	4	5	6	7	0
2	2	3	4	5	6	7	0	1
3	3	4	5	6	7	0	1	2
4	4	5	6	7	0	1	2	3
5	5	6	7	0	1	2	3	4
6	6	7	0	1	2	3	4	5
7	7	0	1	2	3	4	5	6

×	0	1	2	3	4	5	6	7
0	0	0	0	0	0	0	0	0
1	0	1	2	3	4	5	6	7
2	0	2	4	6	0	2	4	6
3	0	3	6	1	4	7	2	5
4	0	4	0	4	0	4	0	4
5	0	5	2	7	4	1	6	3
6	0	6	4	2	0	6	4	2
7	0	7	6	5	4	3	2	1

To divide using the multiplication table, e.g. $4 \div 3$, find 3 down the side of the table, then 4 along this row, and read up the column to the top; the answer is 4. Hence $4 \div 3 = 4$ (modulo 8). However, with division an interesting situation can arise where more than one answer is possible, giving a solution set of numbers, e.g. $4 \div 2 = 2$ or 5 (modulo 8) and $4 \div 4 = 1, 3, 5$ or 7 (modulo 8).

Examination of the numbers in the tables will show that they are the remainders when the result of any operation is divided by the modulo number. For example, if 5 and 7 are added, the arithmetical answer is 12; this is now divided by 8, giving a remainder of 4, so that $5 + 7 = 4$ (modulo 8). Similarly, $6 \times 5 = 30$ by ordinary arithmetic; divide by 8 and the remainder is 6. So $6 \times 5 = 6$ (modulo 8).

As stated earlier, there are important extensions of this work, but this is beyond the scope of this present book. The above work, if done in primary schools, is mainly an interest topic.

INDEX

N.B. *Topics are printed* **bold** *and page numbers where terms are defined,* **bold.**

N.B. *Topics are printed* **bold** *and page numbers where terms are defined,* **bold.**

N.B. *Topics are printed* **bold** *and page numbers where terms are defined,* **bold.**

N.B. *Topics are printed* **bold** *and page numbers where terms are defined,* **bold.**

N.B. *Topics are printed* **bold** *and page numbers where terms are defined,* **bold.**

N.B. *Topics are printed* **bold** *and page numbers where terms are defined,* **bold.**

S

T

U

N.B. *Topics are printed* **bold** *and page numbers where terms are defined,* **bold.**